ROMANTIC KEEPSAKES

ROMANTIC KEEPSAKES

Exquisite heirlooms to create, give and treasure

LUCINDA GANDERTON

PHOTOGRAPHS BY DEBBIE PATTERSON

Sterling Publishing Co., Inc.   New York

For my parents, Colin and Mary Ganderton

Produced by
Anness Publishing Limited
1 Boundary Row
London SE1 8HP

Library of Congress/CIP information available.

Lucinda Ganderton

10 9 8 7 6 5 4 3 2 1

Published 1995 by Sterling Publishing Company, Inc.
387 Park Avenue South, New York, NY 10016

Distributed in Canada by Sterling Publishing
c/o Canadian Manda Group. P.O. Box 920, Station U
Toronto, Ontario, Canada, M8Z 5P9

Printed and bound in Hong Kong

ISBN 0-8069-0801-7

Measurements
Both imperial and metric measurements have been given in the text. Where conversions produce
an awkward number, these have been rounded for convenience, but will produce an accurate
result if one system is followed throughout.

Contents

Introduction

A keepsake is a very special present which has been carefully chosen as a token of friendship and is kept as a treasured memento of the giver. When that gift has been handmade it is valued even more highly. This book contains an inspiring and irresistible treasure trove of ideas, featuring over 40 different romantic gifts. There is something to suit everybody and to mark every occasion when presents are exchanged.

Traditional Gifts

The time, care and skill invested in creating an individual handmade present represent a unique expression of love for the recipient, as well as giving pleasure to the person who makes it. The gifts in Romantic Keepsakes *have been designed to cover a wide range of techniques from dressmaking, patchwork and quilting to simple stitchery and basic embroidery. Some do not involve any sewing at all and many can be made in an afternoon; others will take longer and their challenge will delight the experienced needleworker.*

There are numerous presents to choose from in this book, intended to mark family occasions such as weddings and christenings, special days for individuals such as birthdays, Valentine's Day or Mother's Day, as well as the great celebrations at Christmas. Remember that there is no need for an excuse to give somebody a present: surprises always give great pleasure.

All the projects are carefully explained, with photographs to show clearly each stage of how they are made, and the final chapter provides all the necessary templates and patterns. Most of the projects do not require any special equipment and can be made using the everyday contents of the sewing basket, but do look out for old textiles, or salvage the material from pieces past their best. There is also an illustrated guide to the various stitches and sewing techniques used.

Instructions are given for making gifts ranging from traditional items, such as the christening outfit and wedding quilt, which

Above: Ephemera has always been treasured as a reminder of the past.

have a timeless appeal, and curiosities like the rediscovered Victorian fashion for catch-all gift bags, to new interpretations of favourite themes, such as padded coathangers, hatboxes and shoe-trees. There are also suggestions for innovative ways of arranging dried flowers and many ideas for practical accessories such as the jewellery box and fabric-lined basket. Finally there are items that are purely frivolous and

decorative, such as the hatpins, pincushion and scented cushions.

The textile arts are traditionally a means of demonstrating care and companionship and women have always used the materials they found to hand for making presents for their friends and family. In the past they would show their feelings of affection for loved ones by stitching personal tokens – album quilts, friendship samplers and pincushions – as special gifts.

One of the first histories of embroidery was *The Art of Needlework* published in 1840, when decorative needlework and fancy work were important accomplishments for wealthy women and plain sewing a basic necessity at all social levels. Its author, Elizabeth Stone, wrote of "those numberless pretty and useful tokens of remembrance which, passing from friend to friend, soften our hearts by the feelings they convey". This is an idea that is as appropriate for today's gifts as it was in the nineteenth century and the romantic gifts in this book continue this tradition of present giving.

Left: A workbox should contain the basic sewing tools: a good range of needles, large and small scissors, sharp pins, tailor's chalk, sewing and tacking (basting) cottons, a tape measure, and beeswax to strengthen thread.

Right: A selection of sewing threads and spare buttons are always useful. Mother-of-pearl and fabric-covered buttons can be bought second-hand.

Above: Scraps of fabric, silk flowers and photographs may be used as inspiration for your home-made keepsakes.

Left: Collect swatches of cloth, postcards, magazine cuttings and old photographs to build up a scrapbook of ideas for fabrics, patterns and colour schemes.

FABRICS

In ancient times, when sumptuous fabrics were brought along the Silk Route from the Orient, silk was so valued that it was literally worth its weight in gold, and worn only by the very wealthiest in society. Satins, brocades, organzas, chintz, velvets and taffetas still have an aura of luxury and are the ideal materials from which to make the most special gifts.

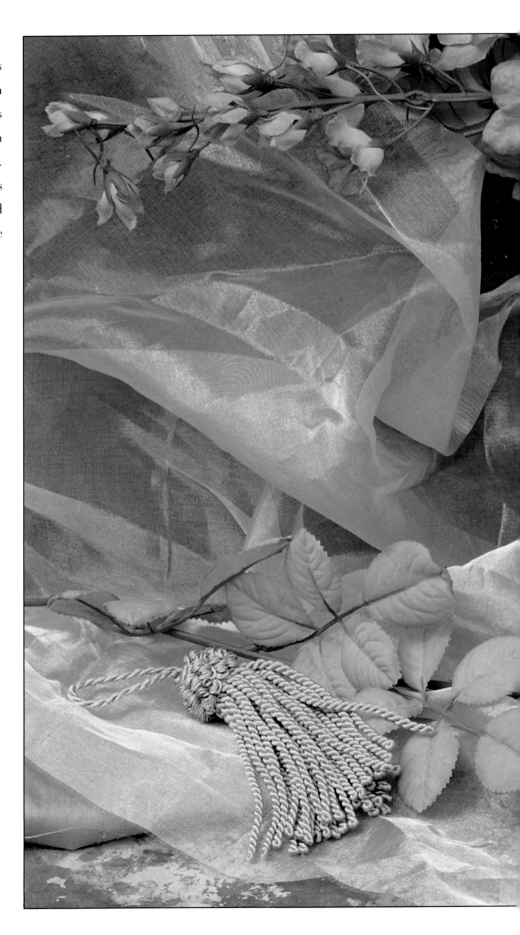

Right: Draw inspiration from the interplay of textures and colours when selecting fabrics.

TRIMMINGS

Carefully selected silk flowers, lace, braids, ribbons, sequins, pearls, beads and buttons can all be used to bring the final decorative touch to a piece of needlework, and are to be found in an infinite diversity. Choose colours and textures to contrast with or match the main fabrics, and use beads and ribbons to highlight or add detail.

Right: Remnants of trims and lace, one-off buttons and spare beads can all be used as delightful trimmings.

In the Bedroom

A bedroom is the most intimate room in the house, a private sanctuary where routine cares can be left behind at the end of the day. It is also the place where clothes are kept, so the projects in this chapter include pretty and practical ways to store and care for garments, shoes and accessories, as well as luxurious gifts to create an atmosphere of comfort.

R o m a n t i c   R e t r e a t s

The sitting- and dining-rooms in a house are on display, but the bedroom is a place to indulge one's own most

personal romantic and decorative dreams. It is the room in which we spend about one-third of our lives, so

bear this in mind when making presents for the bedroom and choose sumptuous fabrics: brocades, satins, braids

and taffetas, or cool madras checks, ginghams or linens.

*I*n the sixteenth century, the English poet Sir Philip Sidney wrote about the delights of ". . . smooth pillows, sweetest bed, a chamber deaf to noise and blind to light". A calm and peaceful bedroom is still essential for a good night's sleep, but in retrospect, an Elizabethan bed would not seem very comfortable to us today. Until the development of wire springs, most mattresses were filled with straw or horsehair and therefore liable to get damp. Copper warming-pans, filled with glowing embers had to be placed under the covers to dry out the bedclothes and to repel bedbugs.

Mrs Beeton, the doyenne of Victorian domesticity, gave detailed advice on how a housemaid should make the bed and clean the bedroom. The mattress had to be turned and the feather mattresses which lay on top had to be vigorously shaken into shape. These were then covered with underblankets, blankets, sheets, a bolster and pillows, before being draped with a counterpane. The maid would be assisted by the kitchen-maid in this task, but she

Above: White cotton pillowcases, trimmed with lace frills, look decorative during the day, and help to induce sweet dreams at night.

also had to clean the room thoroughly each day, including dusting, polishing the mirrors, cleaning the candlesticks and emptying the washstand basin.

BEDLINEN

In larger households, the bedlinen was cared for by the laundry-maid who washed

it all with soap, rinsed it in soda, then dried, mangled and pressed everything with a flat iron to produce a smooth and glossy finish. Sheets and pillowcases were stored in linen chests, with sachets of sweet-scented herbs placed between them to perfume the fabric and to deter moths. Fortunately, this strenuous process has long been superseded by the advent of duvets and tumbledriers, but the freshness of scented sheets can be re-created by adding a few drops of lavender essential oil to the steam iron, or by hanging a lavender bag in the airing cupboard.

An authentic bedroom from the Victorian period would probably appear over-decorated and cluttered to our modern tastes. It must, however, be remembered that the bedroom also had to serve as a place for personal washing, so the furniture had to include a marble washstand, ewer and basin and towel rail.

Nineteenth-century windows were draped with curtains, nets, pelmets (valances), tiebacks and swags; but with coal fires being the only means of warmth, these were necessary for keeping in the heat as

Above: Beaded evening bags were made in a great variety of styles and shapes, and were just big enough to carry perfume, a handkerchief and a dance card. Some were made with tiny matching purses for holding a few coins.

Above: Padded coathangers make a luxurious hanger for a favourite dress, and are too pretty to be hidden away.

Left: These brocade bedroom slippers have a Louis heel and are trimmed with turquoise ostrich feathers. They are typical of the glamour inspired by Hollywood films in the 1930s.

well as being decorative. Even the nets and lace curtains had a secondary function: they kept out insects and, in the industrial towns, airborne factory grime, in addition to maintaining privacy. Today, they can still be used to conceal the view through the window, and to give a light, airy atmosphere to the room setting.

LACE

All kinds of lace can be used to add a nostalgic period touch to even the most modern-style bedroom. Small round crocheted mats and runners can often be found in antique shops and, on a larger scale, lace-edged sheets have a country cottage charm, especially when teamed with a patchwork bedcover. Filet crochet is ideal for making edgings as it will stand up well to regular washing. In Europe, separate turnbacks were traditionally made from cotton sheeting and folded over the top of the bedspread. These were often embroidered with loving messages such as "sleep well", "sweet dreams" or "good night".

The right choice of fabrics can greatly enhance the atmosphere of the bedroom. A grand bedchamber would once have been highly decorated with wall hangings, and would perhaps contain a four-poster bed with curtains, a valance, cushions and pillows which would all have been made from embroidered cloth and tapestry. Textiles in different weights and textures are still important in giving an air of opulence to bedrooms, and cushions in particular are a quick, easy way to enliven a room. They can

Above: Bandboxes got their name from the men's collar bands they were originally made to contain. This set has been covered with hand-blocked American wallpaper for an authentic Colonial feel.

be heaped up on a daybed or chair, or placed among pillows on the bed. As they do not have to stand up to heavy use, upholstery and dressmaking fabrics can be mixed to produce a selection of richly textured covers which can then be trimmed with lavish tassels and fringes.

ACCESSORIES

In the 1920s there was a craze for languorous "boudoir dolls", dressed as fashionable ladies of the day, which would be placed on a bedside chair or arranged as though they happened to be lounging on the bed. The rag doll featured on pages 42–45 would make an elegant ornament, sitting alongside a pile of cushions.

As well as being a place to sleep, the bedroom is also a place for storage, and is furnished with chests of drawers, cupboards and a dressing table primarily for this purpose. Many new homes have built-in units for clothing, but old-fashioned wardrobes, with their separate drawers and compartments for different items, have great appeal. These were often lined with fragrant cedarwood to repel moths. Small cedarwood balls or sandalwood essential oil can now be bought to place in drawers.

Padded coathangers help to keep the shoulders of tailored jackets and dresses in shape, and shoe-trees should always be used to keep leather from distorting with wear. Clothes and shoes are easily stored away in cupboards, but smaller items can sometimes be more of a problem to keep in order. Large, round hatboxes provide a practical solution; they are useful for underwear, gloves, scarves, and other small accessories, as well as hats. When covered in fabric or wallpaper to match the bedroom decor, and stacked upon each other, they also can look very attractive.

Shaker-style wooden boxes provide an excellent means of storage for jewellery, hair accessories and cosmetics. Their distinctive oval shape has made them a design classic, although they were originally intended for the kitchen, as containers for dry goods such as flour, beans and lentils. Cheaper cardboard versions, known as bandboxes, are also available. These are rather less elongated in shape, but can also be decorated and stacked.

Left: Brooch cushions like this Edwardian version would be set out on the dressing table to display treasured pieces of jewellery. This idea is easy to copy today.

Below: These days, hats are worn mainly for formal occasions such as weddings and garden parties but summer straw hats are becoming increasingly fashionable as a desirable protection from the damaging effects of hot sun.

Shoe Bag

*O*ld-fashioned shoe bags are invaluable while travelling, to protect shoes when they are packed in a suitcase. They also look attractive simply hanging on the bedroom door, and can easily be made up from leftover curtain or upholstery material to match the rest of the decor. This simple drawstring shape can easily be adapted in size and made with a waterproof lining for a make-up or wash-bag.

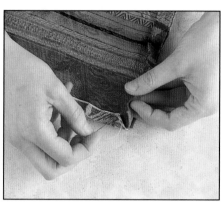

Materials:

24 x 20in (60 x 50cm) upholstery
fabric

matching sewing thread

safety pin

1yd (1m) cord

1 tassel

1 Cut out two rectangles of fabric 12 x 20in (30 x 50cm). Press under ¹⁄₂in (12mm) at one short end on each piece. Place right sides together and pin. Stitch round three sides, starting and finishing 5in (12cm) from the folded edges.

2 Press under ¹⁄₂in (12mm) along the raw edges on each side, unfolding and mitring the corners. Tack (baste), then stitch down, ¹⁄₄in (6mm) from the edge.

3 Double over the two flaps and press. Sew down to the main bag with two parallel rows of straight stitch, ³⁄₄in (18mm) apart, and ¹⁄₄in (6mm) from the edge of flap. This will form a gathering channel for the drawstring. Fasten a small safety pin to one end of the cord and pull it through the channel.

4 Stitch the two cord ends together, and sew on the tassel, so that the tassel loop neatly covers the ends of the cord.

Scented Shoe-trees

A pair of decorative shoe-trees makes a present that is both pretty and practical. The basic shoe-tree is lightly padded, and then covered with a lavender-filled taffeta or silk bag for a long-lasting natural fragrance. Choose fabrics to co-ordinate with a favourite pair of shoes; the variation shown here uses a richly woven brocade ribbon, cream braid and lace.

Materials:

pair of shoe-trees

10 x 20in (25 x 50cm) polyester wadding (batting)

matching sewing thread

6 x 20in (15 x 50cm) taffeta or raw silk

2yd x ½in (1.8m x 12mm) braid

2oz (50g) dried lavender

12 x 1in (30 x 2.5cm) lace

18 x 1in (45 x 2.5cm) ribbon

1 *Cut a small rectangle of wadding (batting) to cover the "heel" of the shoe-tree and bind it in place with sewing thread. Cut a larger piece to cover the toe and attach in the same way.*

2 *Draw around the heel to make a pattern for the heel cover. Using this as a guide, cut out two pieces of taffeta or silk, adding ⅛in (3mm) seam allowance. Sew the pieces together around the curved edge and clip curves. Turn inside out and fit over the padded heel. Run a gathering thread around the raw edge and draw up.*

3 *Make a bag to fit over the toe in the same way as the heel cover. Turn under the seam allowance and run a gathering thread around the open edge. Cut the braid in half. Stitch the end of one length to the heel cover and spiral-wrap tightly along the handle. Secure with a few stitches at the other end.*

4 *Slip the cover over the padded toe and stuff firmly with dried lavender. Draw up the gathering thread and fasten off. Cover the join between toe and handle with a 6in (15cm) ruffle of lace. Stitch the ends together and sew a ribbon rose (see page 26) to the front.*

Padded Coathangers

These lace-covered hangers are far too glamorous to be kept hidden away in the wardrobe. Transform plain wooden coathangers by trimming them with satin, lace, ribbons and roses to go with a special evening gown. Experiment with different fabric combinations – floral cotton prints would be suitable for a summer dress, and a lace and ivory silk hanger would make the perfect present for a bride.

Materials:

8 x 18in (20 x 45cm) satin

wooden coathanger

6 x 18in (15 x 45cm) polyester wadding (batting)

matching sewing thread

6 x 22in (15 x 55cm) lace fabric

1yd x 2½in (1m x 6cm) ribbon

silk rose with leaves

1 Cut a 2 x 18in (5 x 45cm) bias strip of satin, joining several pieces together if necessary. Fold in half and press. Secure one end to the hook with a few stitches, then wind round the hook tightly, to cover the metal completely. Trim any surplus fabric and sew down the end.

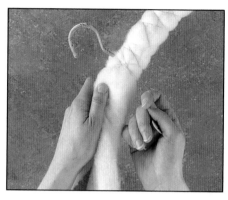

2 Wrap the wadding (batting) around the hanger, overlapping the ends, and bind in place with sewing thread. Cut a small hole in the centre of the satin and fit over the hook. Fold under a narrow hem along one long edge and stretch over the other side of the fabric. Pin together along the bottom of hanger. Box the corners, mitring neatly, and pin.

3 Cut a small hole in the centre of the lace fabric and fit over the hook. Sew the sides together along the underside with whip stitch, removing the pins one at a time. Mitre the lace around the ends of the hanger and sew in place.

4 Make a bow from the ribbon and sew on to the base of the hook. Cut the silk rose and leaves from the wire stalk, if necessary, and sew firmly to the neck of the hanger.

R o s e   H a i r   A c c e s s o r y

*R*ibbon roses are surprisingly straightforward to make and can be used to trim a wide range of gift items and sewing projects. The choice of harmonizing colours in a variety of ribbon widths gives a charming posy effect to this hair accessory, which would be ideal for a young bridesmaid. A fabric-covered hairband could also be decorated with a row of flowers or a straight bar clip could be trimmed with pearls.

Materials:

20 x 1½in (50 x 4cm) cream lace

4in (10cm) oval hairslide (barette)

PVA (white) glue

8 x ⅛in (20cm x 3mm) pale green ribbon

8 x ⅛in (20cm x 3mm) each, pale pink, dark rose pink and beige ribbon

for the roses:

sewing thread in matching colours

32 x 1in (80 x 2.5cm) warm beige ribbon

30 x 1in (75 x 2.5cm) dark rose pink ribbon

20 x ½in (50cm x 12mm) pale pink ribbon

12 x ⅜in (30 x 1cm) cream ribbon

24 x ¼in (60cm x 6mm) dark rose pink ribbon

12 x ¼in (30cm x 6mm) dark pink ribbon

1 *To make a ribbon rose, thread a needle with matching thread and have this standing by for the final step. Fold the ribbon at a right angle, two-thirds along its length and hold in place.*

2 *Pass the long end under the triangular fold and hold with your other hand. Pass the short end under, then continue to make concertina folds to the end of the ribbon.*

3 *Hold the two ends together, and gently grip with the thumb and forefinger of one hand. Carefully draw up the long end. This ruffles the ribbon and forms the rose petals.*

4 *Still holding the rose, make several stab stitches, being sure to pass through all the layers of ribbon. Fasten off the thread and trim the ends of the ribbon.*

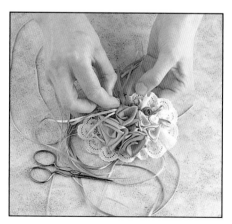

5 *Gather the lace along the straight edge and draw up to fit on to the hairslide (barette). Tucking the raw ends neatly under, glue in place with PVA (white) glue and leave to dry.*

6 *Following the method given, make the roses: one warm beige, two large dark rose pink, three pale pink, two cream, one small dark rose pink, three dark pink. Arrange the roses inside the gathered lace and stick in place, one at a time, with the larger roses towards the centre.*

7 *Cut several 1½in (4cm) lengths of the green ribbon and stitch the ends together to form loops. Sew these between the roses along one outer edge. Make loops and streamers from the rest of the narrow ribbons and attach as shown.*

Hatbox

*H*atboxes make ideal storage containers in the bedroom for all sorts of items besides hats. The basic round boxes can be bought from stationery or gift shops and, with a little imagination, the possibilities for decoration are endless. The flamboyant grape-trimmed box is covered with sari fabric and the green variation is trimmed with fringing, cord, and gold printed paper ribbon.

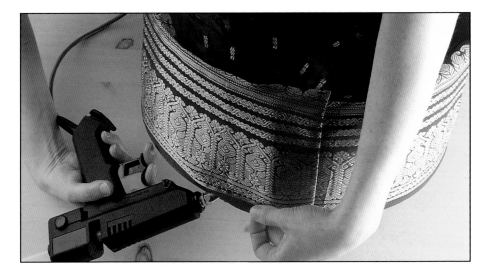

Materials:

14in (36cm) diameter hatbox

1½yd x 45in (1.5m x 115cm) patterned fabric

glue gun or contact adhesive

2yd (1.8m) heavy gold cord

thin card (cardboard)

16 x 36in (40 x 90cm) lining fabric

15 x 30in (38 x 75cm) polyester wadding (batting)

matching sewing thread

1yd x 4in (1m x 10cm) ribbon

2yd x 4in (1.8m x 10cm) wire-edged ribbon

3 bunches artificial grapes

2 gold tassels

1 Cut a length of patterned fabric slightly longer than the circumference of the box and 2½ times its height. Press under ½in (12mm) along one short side, then glue the fabric to the box using a glue gun or impact adhesive. Overlap the folded edge to make a neat join.

2 With the point of a pair of scissors, make a small hole ⅔ of the way up each side. Cut a 30in (75cm) length of gold cord, and insert through the holes to form a carrying handle. Knot securely on the inside and glue in position if necessary.

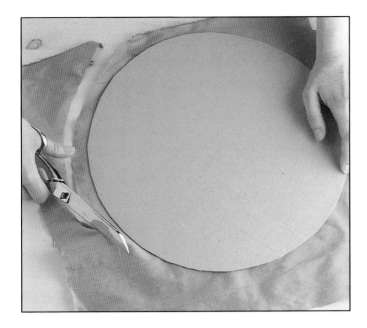

3 *Cut a circle from card (cardboard) measuring ¹/₂in (12mm) less in diameter than the base of the box. Cut out a slightly larger circle of lining fabric and use it to cover one side of the card. Smooth the fabric to prevent any wrinkles forming, then turn over and glue down the edges.*

4 *Fold the excess patterned fabric into the box to line the inside, smoothing the fabric so it lies neatly. Stick the covered circle to the base of the box, with the fabric-covered side uppermost. Any surplus lining fabric will be hidden underneath the card circle.*

5 *Cut a circle of wadding (batting) to fit the outside of the box lid and glue in place. Cover the lid with a strip of the remaining fabric, slightly longer than the circumference of the box lid, and slightly longer than the radius. Glue it around the outside and make a neat join.*

6 *Run a gathering thread through the fabric 7in (18cm) from the rim edge, draw up tightly and neatly, and secure.* ▶

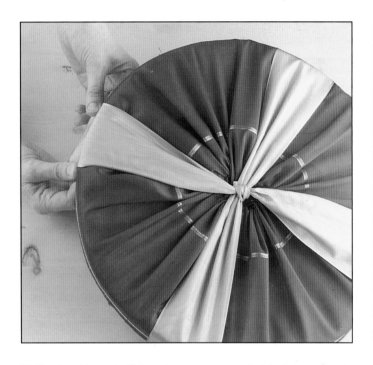

7 *Cut the ribbon in half. Stretch one piece across the lid, gluing each end to the inside of the rim. Knot the other piece on at the centre, then stretch it across the lid at right angles to the first piece. Stick securely in place, smoothing the ribbon to ensure no wrinkles.*

8 *Glue gold cord around the outside of the rim. Butt the two ends together and cover with a narrow strip of fabric to neaten the join.*

9 *Make a bow from the wire-edged ribbon. Cut a "V" shape into the ends and shape the loops. Glue to the centre of the lid, then stick on the three bunches of grapes.*

10 *Finish off by sewing a tassel to each side at the point where the carrying handle joins the box.*

Drawstring Bag

*L*ong-hoarded fragments of antique silk, lace, sequins, beads and silver tassels are combined with new fabrics to make this beautiful jewel-encrusted evening bag, which would make any night out into a special occasion. Time spent scouring flea markets and second-hand shops will yield all kinds of old materials, many of which are ideal for this delightfully informal style of embroidery.

Materials:

18 x 36in (45 x 90cm) cream silk or cotton fabric for backing lace and lining bag

10 x 36in (25 x 90cm) gold gauze

10 x 36in (25 x 90cm) lace fabric

matching sewing thread

contrasting metallic lace

selection of beads, pearls and sequins

scraps of ribbon and lace

gold cord

bodkin

thin card (cardboard)

2 silver tassels

1 *Cut out two pieces each of cream silk or cotton, gauze and lace measuring 12 x 10in (30 x 25cm) for the sides of the bag and a 5½in (14cm) diameter circle in each fabric for the base. Tack (baste) the three layers together with the lace on top, then the gauze, then the silk or cotton.*

2 *Cut out several motifs from the metallic lace and pin and sew to the lace fabric, spacing them at random.*

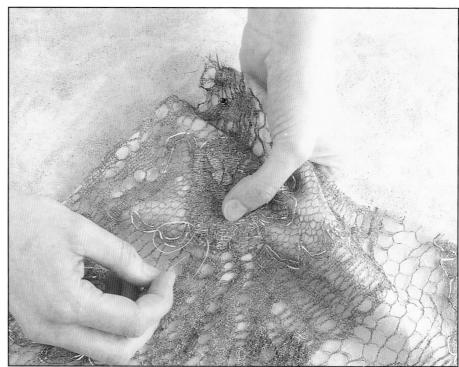

3 *Make a channel for the drawstring by folding over 3in (7.5cm) fabric at the short end of each side and sewing two rows of stitches ¾in (18mm) apart around the lower edge of the turnback. Hand- or machine-stitch the two sides together, as far as the drawstring channel, then sew on the base. Turn in the raw edges of the drawstring channel and slip stitch the sides.*

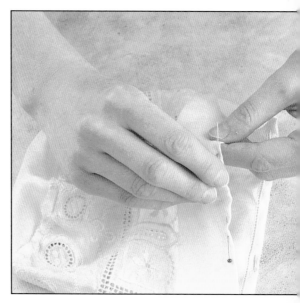

5 *To make the lining, cut two pieces of silk or cotton 6½ x 8½in (16.5 x 21cm) and a circle 5in (12cm) in diameter. Join the sides and sew on the base.* ▶

4 *Decorate the bag with a random pattern of beads, pearls, sequins and tiny scraps of ribbon* *and lace, sewing them on firmly and leaving the channel for the drawstring free.*

6 *Take the completed lining, and with wrong sides together, slip the lining over the embroidered bag. Pin the lining just below the drawstring channel to ensure the drawstring will move freely and slip stitch in place.*

7 *Cut two 25in (63cm) lengths of cord and thread through the channel with a bodkin.*

8 *Cut four 1in (2.5cm) circles of card (cardboard) to make the tassel tops. Cut four circles of gauze slightly larger than the card circles. Cover the circles with the gauze and finish on the wrong side with gathering thread. Decorate with beads.*

9 *Sew the ends of the cord and the top of the tassel to one circle, then overstitch to the second circle. Repeat for the other drawstring.*

Pouch Bag

$\mathscr{T}$he colour and texture of this evening bag are reminiscent of a peacock's lavish tail feathers. The looped fringe is ingeniously made from narrow ribbon, and gold thread and cord are used to decorate the green velvet pouch. This project requires a swing-needle sewing machine and makes a good introduction to basic machine embroidery techniques, as it is fairly straightforward to create.

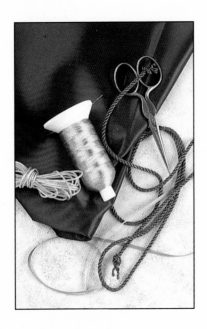

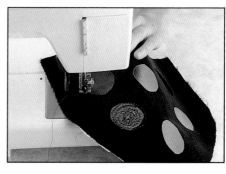

Materials:

12 x 36in (30 x 90cm) dark green velvet

12 x 36in (30 x 90cm) lining

12 x 36in (30 x 90cm) iron-on interfacing

4in (10cm) iron-on bonding fabric

4 x 20in (10 x 50cm) satin

gold thread

dark green sewing thread

2¾yd (2.5m) thin gold cord

1½yd (1.5m) green cord

7¾yd x ⅛in (7m x 3mm) green ribbon

1 Cut out the bag pieces to the size required, allowing a ½in (1cm) seam allowance, two from velvet, two from the lining and one from interfacing. Iron the interfacing to the wrong side of the velvet. Iron the bonding fabric to the wrong side of the satin and cut out 12 1½in (4cm) circles. Remove the backing paper. Lay the circles at random on the velvet and press.

2 Wind the machine spool (bobbin) with gold thread and loosen the spoolcase (bobbin case) tension by turning the screw. Lower the feed teeth (clogs) and release the tension on the pressure foot. Fit an embroidery foot to the machine. Using straight stitch, sew spirals on to the satin, letting the gold thread loop up from underneath.

3 Reset the machine and load the spool with dark green thread. Tighten the screw on the spoolcase until the thread can just support its weight. Using the cording foot, zig-zag the gold and green cords in place between the circles. Use straight stitch to sew the ribbon in place.

4 Cut two 1½in (4cm) wide strips of paper and fold in half lengthways. Wrap the ribbon round the paper, spacing it evenly. Sew a line ⅛in (3mm) from one edge, then tear out the paper. Pin and tack (baste) the fringe around the embroidered panel. Sew seven small loops of ribbon along the top of both bag panels.

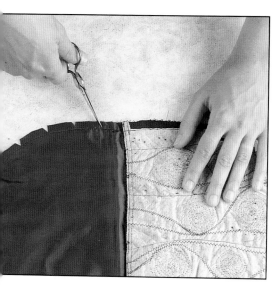

5 *Join the lining pieces to the bag panels along the straight edge, trim the seam and press flat. Straight stitch along the top edge to hold the seam in place. With right sides facing, sew the two oval-shaped pieces together, leaving a 3in (7.5cm) gap at the lining end. Trim ⅛in (3mm), leaving a seam allowance, and notch the curves before turning through the gap. Sew invisibly with stab stitch along the top edge to hold the lining in place.*

6 *Thread gold cord through the loops and tie a knot at each end. Sew four loops to each end and wrap ribbon round to form a tassel. Sew in place.*

C u s h i o n s

*T*hese opulent cushions are covered in velvet, moiré taffeta and brocade, and trimmed with fringing, tassels and woven upholstery braid. Despite their extravagant appearance, they are relatively simple to construct, without requiring any complicated sewing techniques or difficult piping. Whether piled up on an armchair, or stacked on a bed, they offer an invitation to relax in comfort.

SQUARE CUSHION

Materials:

1yd x 20in (1m x 50cm) velvet

10in (25cm) square moiré taffeta

matching sewing thread

1¾yd x 3in (1.6m x 7.5cm) woven braid

20in (50cm) square pillow form

2yd (1.8m) heavy cord

1 *Cut the velvet in half to make two squares. Place the taffeta square in the centre of one of the velvet pieces, pin, then tack (baste) in place.*

2 *Border the taffeta with the woven braid, carefully mitring the corners, then pin, tack and stitch down in place.*

3 *With right sides facing, sew the two velvet squares together around three sides. Clip the corners, turn inside out and place the pillow form inside the cover. Turn the raw edges under and slip stitch the open sides together, leaving a 1in (2.5cm) gap at one corner.*

4 *Tuck one end of the cord inside the gap, stitch in place, then attach it around the outside edge of the cushion with slip stitch. Make a small loop of cord at each corner and, when the final corner is reached, hide the end of the cord inside the gap. Secure the end and stitch up the gap.*

BOLSTER CUSHION

1 Cut the silk and organza fabrics in half. Join one piece of silk and one of organza along one long edge and then sew to the moiré taffeta with the organza facing the taffeta. Repeat with the second pieces of silk and organza, attaching them to the other long edge of the taffeta. ◄

2 Cut the woven braid in half. Pin, tack (baste) and sew to the fabric to cover the two seam lines. Press lightly with a cool iron. ▼

Materials:

32 x 25in (80 x 63cm) silk

32 x 25in (80 x 63cm) gold spotted organza

16 x 25in (40 x 63cm) moiré taffeta

matching sewing thread

50 x 3in (126 x 7.5cm) woven braid

18in (45cm) bolster pillow form

2 x 1¼in- (3cm-) wide self-cover buttons

2 tassels

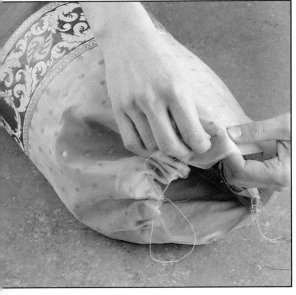

3 Sew the long ends together to form a tube. Turn inside out and place the pillow form inside the cover. Using double thread, run a gathering stitch around each end, draw up, tuck the raw edges to the inside and finish off. ◄

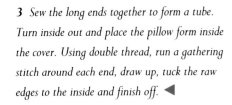

4 Following the manufacturer's instructions, cover the two self-cover buttons with taffeta. Sew on to the centre of each round end of the bolster and finish off with a tassel at each end. ►

ROUND CUSHION

1 *Cut fourteen 14 x 4½in (36 x 11cm) strips from the assorted fabrics. Sew together along the long edges to make a single strip, alternating the colours, then join the ends to make a tube. Press the seams so that they lie flat.* ◀

2 *Run a thread along one edge, and gather to fit around the circle of velvet. Pin in position, right sides together, adjusting the gathers evenly. Tack (baste) and stitch in place.* ▼

Materials:

assorted remnants of brocade, or old upholstery fabric sample book

matching sewing thread

12in (30cm) diameter circle of matching velvet

18in (45cm) round pillow form

2in (5cm) button

1½yd x 5in (1.5m x 12cm) heavy fringing

3 *Put the pillow inside the cover and gather the other edge. Cut a 3in (7.5cm) circle of brocade, and gather round the outside edge to cover the button. Draw up the thread and finish off tightly. Sew the button to the centre.* ◀

4 *Finish by sewing on the fringing.* ▲

Calico Doll

*T*his elegantly costumed rag doll will appeal to all ages. Her hair is styled into ringlets, and she is dressed for a Victorian summer in a cotton dress and flower garlanded straw hat. Underneath she wears a full set of lawn (fine cotton) underclothes, complete with a tightly-laced pink corset. If the doll is to be given to a child, both hair and accessories must be made securely childproof.

Materials:

for the doll:

16 x 36in (40 x 90cm) white cotton

1 bag polyester toy stuffing

embroidery threads in black, red, blue, white and pink

12 x 8in (30 x 20cm) thin card (cardboard)

for the clothes:

1yd x 1yd (1m x 1m) fine white lawn (fine cotton)

2yd (1.8m) narrow broderie anglaise (eyelet lace)

matching sewing thread

mother-of-pearl buttons

18 x ⅛in (45 x 3mm) white ribbon

12 x 6in (30 x 15cm) pink satin

1yd x ½in (1m x 12mm) pink ribbon

10 hooks and eyes

18 x ¼in (45cm x 6mm) pink lace

18 x 36in (45 x 90cm) flowered lawn (fine cotton)

1yd (1m) wide broderie anglaise (eyelet lace)

12in (30cm) woven braid for sash

small piece of black felt

2 tiny buckles and short length of blue ribbon

doll's straw hat trimmed with silk flowers

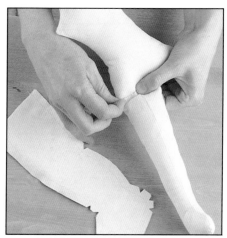

1 *Trace the pattern pieces from pages 147–9, enlarging by 20%. Cut two body pieces and stitch the head darts as marked, allowing a ¼in (6mm) seam. Pin, tack (baste) and stitch* between 'a' and 'a'. Trim the seams, clip the corners and turn right side out. Tack under ½in (12mm) around the open edge. Stuff the body tightly, making sure that the neck is firm.

2 *Cut four leg pieces. Sew together in pairs between 'b' and 'b'. Trim the seams, turn right side out and stuff. Insert into the lower edge of body and stitch in place.*

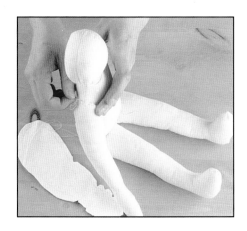

3 Cut four arm pieces and stitch in pairs from 'c' to 'c'. Trim the seams, clip the curves and turn right side out. Stuff lightly and slip stitch the gap to close. Sew in place on the shoulders.

4 Make the ringlets by twisting 6in (15cm) 10-strand skeins of black embroidery thread until they double back. Sew firmly in place around the sides of the head to frame the face. Trim any loose ends.

5 Wind the remaining thread around the card (cardboard). Using black thread, back stitch the strands together along one edge to form the centre parting. Cut the yarn along the other edge. Sew to the head from forehead to nape. Form a bun and stitch in place.

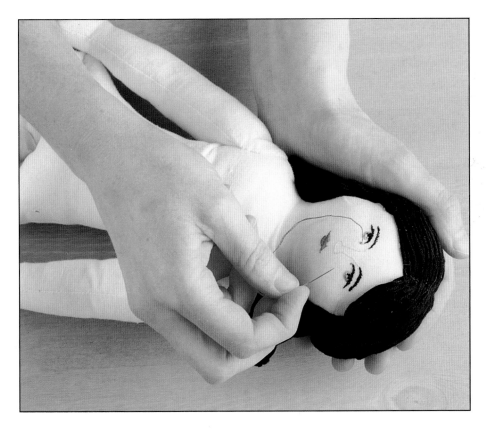

6 Transfer the facial features from the template, marking the lines with a pencil. Embroider the features with single strands of thread. The mouth is worked in red satin stitch. The irises of the eyes are blue satin stitch with a white French knot as a highlight. Using black, work the pupils in satin stitch, eyelids in stem stitch and eyebrows in feather stitch. Outline the nose in pink stem stitch and work a pink French knot at each corner of the inner eyes.

7 Cut two bloomer legs and a 1½ x 9in (4 x 23cm) waistband from white lawn (fine cotton). Join front seam from crotch to waist. Join back seam, leaving 2½in (6cm) open at waist edge. Join inside legs, pin-tuck edges and trim with narrow broderie anglaise (eyelet lace). Sew under the seam allowance on either side of the opening. Gather the top edge to fit the waistband, leaving ½in (12mm) at each end, then sew together. Press under ¼in (6mm) along edge of waistband. Fold in half and slip stitch to cover gathers. Neaten ends, then sew on a button. Make a button hole on the other side. Trim with white ribbon bows. ▶

8 *Cut two chemise pieces from white lawn. Join at shoulder and side seams. Turn under and press seam allowances at neck and sleeve edges, clipping curves. Sew on narrow broderie anglaise edging. Cut opening at back as shown, then turn under and neaten edges. Sew on a button and make a button hole at the neck edge.* ▼

9 *For the petticoat, cut two 20 x 8in (50 x 20cm) and one 6 x 12in (15 x 30cm) rectangles of white lawn. Join the two large pieces at short edges, leaving 3in (7.5cm) unstitched at one end. Neaten edges of this opening. Trim the hem with narrow broderie anglaise. Gather the top edge up to 12in (30cm). Pin to long edge of small rectangle (yoke), even out gathers and* stitch in place. Press under ½in (12mm) around three sides of yoke and fold in half lengthways. Slip stitch together short sides and slip stitch long edge to skirt, covering the raw edges. Gather the waist edge and draw up to 8in (20cm). Make and attach a waistband as for bloomers. Sew a button to one end of band and make a button hole on the other side.* ▲

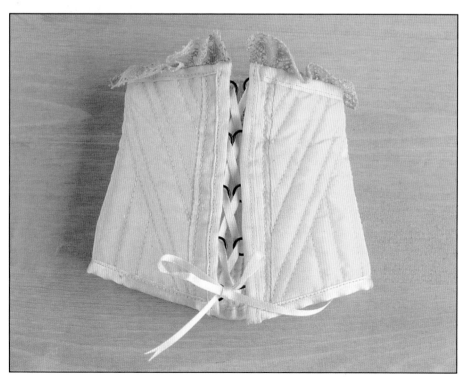

10 *Cut two corset pieces from pink satin. Tack (baste), then stitch together following quilting lines on template. Trim outside edges and bind with ½in (12mm) pink ribbon. Sew five hook and eye loops along each side of front opening and lace up with narrow pink ribbon. Trim the top edge with pink lace.*

11 *Cut one front and two back dress bodices from flowered lawn (fine cotton). Join side and shoulder seams. Turn under ½in (12mm) at the neck and clip the curve. Top stitch down, close to the edge. Press under ½in (12mm) on either side of the back opening. Cut two sleeves. Join side seams then gather the sleeve head. Pin into armhole, tack and sew. Gather the cuff and trim with narrow broderie anglaise. Cut a 1yd x 8in (1m x 20cm) rectangle for the skirt. Sew wide broderie anglaise to the hem, then gather waist to fit lower edge of bodice. Pin in place, even out the gathering and sew. Join sides of skirt to 2in (5cm) from waist and neaten the opening. Sew on buttons and make buttonholes evenly up the back opening, then tie a sash of woven braid around the waist.*

12 *Cut four shoe shapes from black felt. Sew together between the dots, leaving a ¼in (6mm) seam, and trim with ribbon bows and buckles. Sew on to the doll. Add the straw hat.*

Bathroom & Boudoir

Everybody should set aside some time for relaxation, and the best way to do this is by creating your own personal haven from the outside world. A woman's traditional retreat was once her boudoir, a feminine sanctuary where she could pamper herself, surrounded by her favourite possessions, jewellery and lavish furnishings. The projects in this chapter help to recapture something of this atmosphere of luxurious self indulgence.

Private Sanctuaries

The boudoir was originally part of a wealthy woman's suite of rooms, alongside her bedchamber and dressing room. Here she could write her letters and journals, read, or simply daydream, away from the rest of the household. Today, few of us have the luxury of our own special room, and so the bathroom has become a favourite place of escape for many of us; a long soak in a warm bath is a wonderful way to unwind from daily cares, amid the scents of relaxing oils and perfumes.

Cosmetics in the eighteenth century were extremely expensive and their use, therefore, was limited to the few who could afford them. Thus, those with wealth could be clearly distinguished from the rest of society, not just by their ostentatious clothing, but by their facial appearance. A pallid white complexion was considered the height of fashion and was obtained by applying treatments containing ingredients ranging from hydrochloric acid to grapes, whale oil, horseradish, and bitter almonds. Face powders contained chemical compounds of lead, mercury or arsenic, all of which are potentially lethal and damaging to the skin. Cut-out paper patches in the shape of hearts, flowers or diamonds were applied to the face to conceal pockmarks and blemishes, and became a fashionable but necessary conceit. Heavy perfumes were used liberally, mainly to veil the effects of infrequent washing.

A Victorian lady of leisure would spend many hours sitting in front of her looking-glass to perform her toilette, usually

Above: Shells, such as this highly polished one which holds a tiny pincushion, are a favourite theme for bathroom accessories. The lace- and shell-trimmed square box is an extravagant container for a single bath-cube that would make bathtime a very special occasion.

attended by her maid. Fashionable hairstyles were often highly elaborate, with the hair twisted into a series of ringlets, plaits and buns, wound over pads and held in place with hairpins. Most women did not wash their long hair very often, but brushed it vigorously to give it a sheen.

DRESSING TABLES

The nineteenth-century dressing table was an elaborate piece of furniture, with mirrors, small drawers and shelves. These would be filled with the many accessories needed for personal grooming; pin trays, hatpin and ring stands, powder bowls and a jewellery box. Such accessories were often beautifully crafted from precious materials, and might have included silver-backed bristle hairbrushes, tortoiseshell combs, ebony or ivory glove stretchers, crystal perfume bottles and perfume atomizers with silk tassels. The overall effect was one of dazzling extravagance.

Among the useful items on the dressing table would be others that were merely decorative, but of great sentimental value. Silver frames containing sepia photographs of loved ones jostled for space with elaborate beaded pin-stuck cushions, which were highly valued. These were often made

Above: Elaborately embroidered lace handkerchiefs were treated as decorative fashion accessories rather than functional items. This white work example was made in the mid-nineteenth century.

Above: These frivolous powder puffs in female form were made in the 1930s. One has a handle made from a pompadour-style half doll and the other has a saucy pair of shapely legs.

Above: Perfume bottles come in a wide range of colours, shapes and sizes. Old and new bottles can be clustered together to make a fascinating collection on a shelf or windowsill, especially if sunlight can filter through the glass.

49

to commemorate special events. Some, with messages such as "true love" or "think of me" were given as love tokens by bashful suitors enabling them to declare their feelings without having to say anything. These Victorian versions had evolved from the practical pinholders of an earlier age. Before the invention of hooks and eyes or press studs (snaps), pins were vital in holding together voluminous dresses, and a special cushion was necessary to keep them safe.

The nineteenth century saw the advent of mass production and a wide range of perfumes and make-up became available for the first time. Previously, simple beauty preparations had been made at home, and many people continued to use the old recipes for rose- and lavender-waters and hair lotions. These were labelled carefully and stored in fancy moulded or cut-glass bottles. This can easily be emulated today, by decanting shampoos and bath oils into decorative bottles or jars and setting them out on a shelf rather than hiding them away in the bathroom cabinet.

BATHROOM STYLES

The bathroom did not exist in its present form until the late nineteenth century. Until then, bath-night tended to be a weekly event undertaken in an enamel hip bath or tin tub. This would be set up in front of the fire, in the bedrooms of larger houses, or in front of the kitchen range in most homes. It would be filled with jugs of precious hot water, and often the whole family would take turns to wash in the same bathwater.

New developments in sanitation and plumbing meant that mains water could be piped under pressure to all houses and tanks were installed in loft spaces. The smallest bedroom was often adapted to accommodate a large, free-standing roll-top bath on ball-and-claw feet, along with a

washbasin and lavatory. The newly converted room often retained the comforts of the original bedroom – pictures hanging on the walls, an open fireplace, chairs and a table. Without central heating, the bathroom could be a chilly place in winter, somewhere to wash quickly and hurry out

Above: This stylish cushion cover is skilfully machine-embroidered with images of crabs and starfish. The well-chosen colours evoke memories of sunny seaside holidays, and give a bright, contemporary feel.

again. Today, however, it has become a place of warmth and comfort where one can linger. A long hot soak after a strenuous or stressful day is relaxing and indulgent, especially if bubble bath or soothing essential oils are added to the water. Conversely, an invigorating shower is a good way to wake up first thing in the morning.

Scented soaps, perfumed oils, bath beads and other bathtime preparations have long been popular gifts, especially for birthdays and Christmas. Carefully chosen soaps in toning colours can be turned into an individual present by putting them in a small basket which has been specially lined in a matching fabric.

A nautical or seaside theme is a popular choice for decorating the bathroom. Many shops stock tiles, towels and other matching accessories patterned with shells, fish and starfish. Stencilling is ideal for bathrooms, and any of these motifs could easily be adapted to make friezes and borders.

Dried flowers also bring colour to the bathroom, and the warm steamy atmosphere enhances the scent of a bunch of dried lavender or an open bowl of potpourri. The lavender wreath on page 66 could be hung on the back of the door where the constant movement will release the fragrance. The plant has long been associated with the linen cupboard – its name shares the same root, *lavare*, as the word laundry – and its perfume is very long lasting. Sachets of lavender or lavender dollies can be placed between sheets and towels for a nostalgic, soothing freshness.

Left: Traditionally, a bunch of a dozen lavender dollies was exchanged between girlfriends to mark a betrothal. These would be used to add scent to and keep moths from the linen stored in a dowry chest.

Below: Scented bath and body oils can be made at home by adding a few drops of favourite essential oil to a carrying agent, such as almond oil. They look attractive when stored in antique bottles and tied with ribbons.

L i n g e r i e   C a s e

*T*his lingerie case in crisp white cotton is a reminder of an elegant age, when all household linens were starched, ironed and scented with lavender. It is trimmed with a frill and narrow insertion, and is threaded with scarlet ribbon in traditional nineteenth-century style. An alternative use could be as a nightgown case, where it would look attractive on the top of a bed, among lacy pillows.

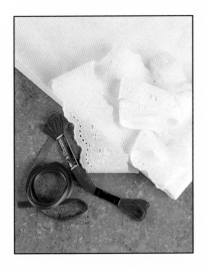

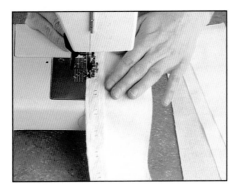

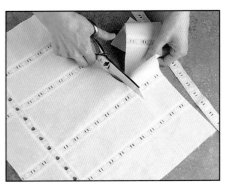

Materials:

2½yd x 18in (2.25m x 45cm) white cotton sheeting

3yd (2.75m) narrow broderie anglaise (eyelet lace) insertion

bodkin

1yd (1m) scarlet ribbon

matching sewing thread

2½yd x 2in (2.25m x 5cm) broderie anglaise edging

scarlet embroidery thread

1 *Cut four rectangles of cotton, each 3 x 18in (7.5 x 45cm) and 1 rectangle measuring 5 x 18in (12 x 45cm). Cut four 18in (45cm) lengths of broderie anglaise (eyelet lace) insertion. Join one of the narrow rectangles to the insertion, allowing a ¼in (6mm) seam, then stitch another narrow rectangle to the other side of the insertion. Sew the other two narrow pieces together in the same way, then join to the large rectangle, again with insertion.*

2 *Press the seams away from the lace. Measure a line 3in (7.5cm) from each long edge of the cover and mark. Cut along these lines, and rejoin the pieces together with remaining insertion. Use a bodkin to thread the ribbon through the insertion on both long sides.*

3 *Join the two ends of the broderie anglaise edging and run a gathering thread along the bottom edge. Pull up to fit around the outside of the cover, allowing fullness at the corners. Pin to right side of cover, so that the lace faces inwards. Tack (baste) in place, ¼in (6mm) from the edge.*

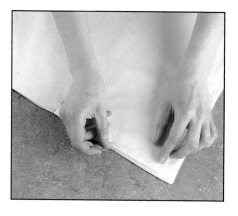

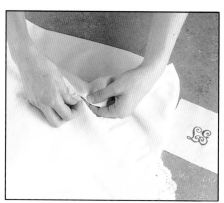

4 *Cut a piece of cotton the same size as the cover and pin to the right side. Tack the two together, then sew ½in (12mm) from the edge, slightly curving the corners and leaving 4in (10cm) gap along one side. Turn right side out and slip stitch the gap. Press so that lace lies flat.*

5 *Make the main bag from a piece of cotton sheeting 18in x 1½yd (45cm x 1.5m). Fold in half and seam around three sides, ½in (12mm) from the edge, leaving a 4in (10cm) gap. Turn inside out and slip stitch the gap. Fold in half again lengthways, and join the short sides ¼in (6mm) from the edge. Turn the bag inside out again, then press lightly.*

6 *Slip stitch the cover to the main bag as shown. An initial or monogram in scarlet thread can be embroidered directly on to one corner or worked on a separate piece of cloth and then sewn in place to add a personal touch.*

Jewellery Box

This regal purple box is covered in jaquard silk and lined with delicate lilac lightweight silk. The lid is quilted, following the pattern of the fabric, and beaded with sparkling starburst motifs to highlight the design. The box has a padded interior, divided into two compartments, which helps to protect precious pieces of jewellery, and allows for brooches to be pinned inside the lid.

Materials:

sheet of ¼in (6mm) foam-core board

cutting board

metal ruler and craft knife

20 x 36in (50 x 90cm) toning
lightweight silk

PVA (white) glue

adhesive tape

8 x 16in (20 x 40cm) calico

thin card (cardboard)

12 x 36in (30 x 90cm) of silk
jaquard fabric

clothes pegs (pins)

matching embroidery silks

40 x 36in (1m x 90cm) polyester
wadding (batting)

embroidery hoop

assortment of small beads

1 Draw up the six box pieces on to the foam-core board: two 6 x 8in (15 x 20cm) rectangles for the lid and base; two 3 x 8in (7.5 x 20cm) sides and two 3 x 5½in (7.5 x 14cm) ends. Cut out on a cutting board using a metal rule and a craft knife. (If you want different dimensions, adjust the pieces as required and allow more or less fabric as appropriate.)

2 Cut four pieces of lining from the lightweight silk, slightly larger than each side and end. Using PVA (white) glue, stick the fabric along each side about half-way down, stretching it tightly. When nearly dry, turn the board over and stretch the silk across the top edge, gluing it to the back. Trim the silk close to the board, leaving a short overlap at each corner. Cover the base piece with lining fabric in the same way.

3 Spread glue along the base of one long side, and along the base and edge of one end. Place the base right-side up and position the two sides around the corner of the base. Glue and place the other two sides around the opposite corner. Use adhesive tape to keep the joints tight while the glue dries. Use a pin to push the silk overlaps at the top corners down into the cracks.

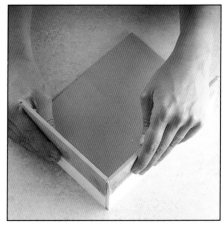

4 *Draw the hinge on to calico: the base should be the width of one long side, plus one end, with the 'flap' slightly smaller than the box lid. Cut the flap sides at an angle as shown. Glue to the box back and around the sides, leaving the flap at the top.*

5 *From thin card (cardboard), cut three rectangles the same size as the front and two sides of the assembled box. Cover each piece with silk jaquard, then glue to the front and sides of the box, holding the fabric in place with clothes pegs (pins) while the glue dries.*

6 *With embroidery silk, overstitch the joins at the box corners, then return along each line of stitching to form cross stitches.* ▲

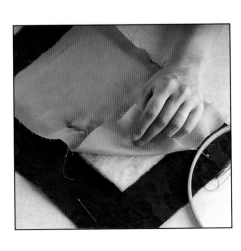

7 *Cut a 10 x 13in (25 x 33cm) piece of jaquard to cover the lid and a piece of wadding (batting) slightly larger than the lid itself. From the lightweight silk, cut out a 7 x 9in (18 x 23cm) rectangle. Sandwich the layers together as shown and put into an embroidery hoop, stretching the fabric tightly.* ◀

8 *Make French knots in a harmonizing colour, stitching through all three layers and picking out details of the jaquard pattern, or creating a random effect. Keeping the piece in the embroidery hoop, quilt the fabric by hand or machine, outlining the shapes within the material.* ▲ ▶

9 *With a contrasting colour and single stitches, sew star shapes around the French knots. Sew beads around the outer edges of the stars, and embroider additional stars in any spaces.* ▼

10 *Position the card for the lid on the wrong side of the embroidery and trim the wadding and backing as necessary. Glue the front face-down,* *stretching the fabric firmly, then stretch and glue the two sides, neatening or mitring the corners. Allow to dry thoroughly.* ▲

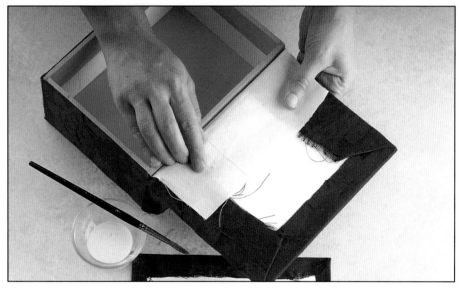

11 *Stick the calico hinge to the underside of the lid so that the lid lies squarely on the box when closed. Cut a piece of card the same size as the back of the box, less ⅛in (3mm) in depth to allow the lid to open properly. Cover with jaquard silk as before. Making sure that the front* *is flush with the box, glue the back flap of the embroidered lid to the back of the box, then glue on the jaquard-covered card. Embroider the corners, as in Step 6, then glue the upper long side of inner hinge to the inside of the lid.*

12 *Cut a piece of thin card slightly smaller than the lid of the box, cover it with lightweight silk, then glue in place on the underside. Cut a piece of card and wadding ½in (12mm) smaller all round than the box lid and lightly glue them together. Stretch and glue the silk over the wadding then stick the card in the centre of the underside of the box lid. Make a centre divider from a silk-covered piece of foam-core board ⅜in (1cm) lower than the walls. Pad the inside of the box by covering and padding pieces of card to fit each wall as for the inside lid, and glue in place.*

Lace Handkerchief

The delicate antique beige colour of this cotton handkerchief is achieved by dipping it in tea. This is a simple and effective dying technique that does not require any special equipment. Experiment with herbal tisanes and fruit teas, which give subtle shades, or coffee, which gives a warmer tone. When old and new materials are used in one project, this method of dying helps the colours blend together.

Materials:

white cotton handkerchief

teabags and boiling water

large basin

tongs

white lace, 1½ times the length of the handkerchief border

3 or 4 embroidered motifs in cotton, or cotton mix

matching sewing thread

1 *Wash the handkerchief so that the dye will take evenly. Make a strong brew of tea with three teabags in a large basin. Allow to cool slightly and remove the teabags. Using the tongs, dip the lace, handkerchief and motifs separately into the tea until they change to a soft beige colour. Rinse in clean water and allow to dry.*

2 *Stitch the motifs to one corner on the right side of the handkerchief. Use tiny stitches so that the work will look neat from the reverse. Press with a cool iron.*

3 *With a long length of sewing thread, run a row of small gathering stitches along the bottom of the lace, as near to the edge as possible.*

4 *Starting a short distance in from one corner, place the lace along the handkerchief edge with right sides together. Oversew the lace on to the hem with tiny stitches, starting ¼in (6mm) from the end. This overlap will be used to join the ends of the lace when the sewing is completed. Adjust the gathers carefully while stitching so that the lace lies evenly.*

5 Ease the lace gently round each corner so that the handkerchief lies flat without being pulled out of shape. ◄

6 Just before reaching the other end of the lace, trim back the two ends to leave a narrow overlap. Oversew together on the wrong side, then complete the stitching, adjusting the gathers of the lace. With a cool iron, press the lace away from the handkerchief on the right side. ▶

Fabric-lined Basket

*T*his country-style wicker basket has been painted and covered with Provençal-style floral-printed cotton to provide useful storage for all the various lotions, pots and tubes that accumulate in the bathroom.

This design is finished with a drawstring cover to conceal what is inside, but an open version makes a pretty place to display more attractively packaged cosmetics.

1 *Smooth down any rough edges on the basket with fine-grade sandpaper, then apply a thin coat of white acrylic paint and leave to dry. Pick a colour to match your fabric and paint the rim and base. Leave to dry, then coat with matt (flat) varnish.*

Materials:

small round basket

fine-grade sandpaper

white and toning acrylic paints

paintbrushes

matt (flat) varnish

floral-printed cotton fabric

matching sewing thread

1yd x 2½in (1m x 6cm) broderie anglaise (eyelet lace)

lining fabric

2yd (1.8m) narrow woven floral braid

bodkin

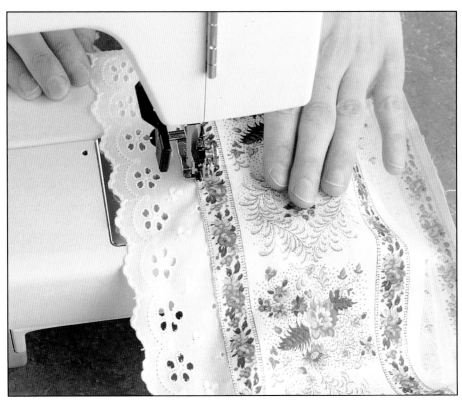

2 *Measure the circumference and radius of the basket. Add on 2in (5cm) to each length and cut a rectangle of floral fabric to this size. Join the short edges together and press the seam open.*

Press under ½in (12mm) along one long side, and top stitch to the broderie anglaise (eyelet lace), half-way down the lace. Join the ends of the broderie anglaise neatly together.

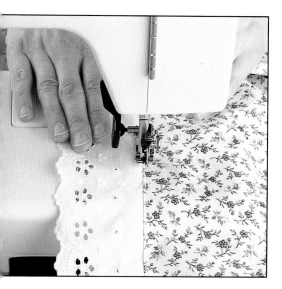

3 *Cut a rectangle of lining to the same length as the floral fabric and three times its width. Join the short edges, then press under ½in (12mm) around one open side. With the wrong sides together, sew the lining to the floral fabric, ½in (12mm) below the previous stitching. This forms a channel for the drawstring.*

4 *Run a gathering thread along the bottom edge of the lining fabric. Gather it up and secure tightly with the excess material on the wrong side. Sew the outside edge of the flowered fabric to the inside rim of the basket. Cut the braid in half and use a bodkin to thread each piece through the gathering channel. Knot the ends together and draw closed.*

J e w e l l e r y   R o l l

A jewellery roll should be part of every woman's luggage set. This luxuriously padded and embroidered velvet version is specially designed to safeguard its contents when travelling. It has a separate zippered compartment for bracelets and necklaces, individual pockets to prevent larger earrings and brooches from getting scratched and a ribbon strap to hold rings in place.

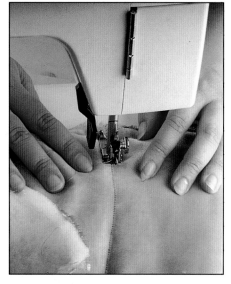

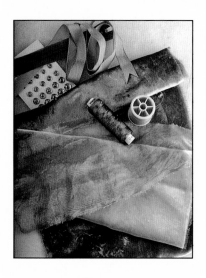

1 *Tack (baste) the wadding (batting) to the wrong side of the outer fabric, smoothing carefully. Sew together round the outside edges and straight stitch across the width 3½in (9cm) from the left edge.*

2 *Draw your chosen design on to tissue paper. Tack the organza to the right side of the velvet and the tissue paper to the wrong side, 3½in (9cm) from the left edge. Straight stitch over the pencil line, working from the wrong side. Turn the piece over, cut back the excess organza, then zig-zag stitch over the outline on the right side, using metallic thread.*

Materials:

9 x 13in (23 x 33cm) polyester wadding (batting)

9 x 13in (23 x 33cm) velvet for outer layer

matching sewing thread

tissue paper

9 x 4in (23 x 10cm) metallic organza

metallic machine-embroidery thread

1¾yd x ¾in (1.6m x 18mm) ribbon

8in (20cm) zip (zipper) in matching colour

9 x 19in (23 x 48cm) contrasting velvet for lining

press studs (snaps)

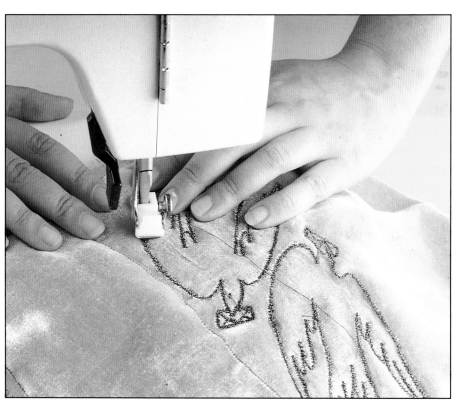

3 *Cut a 9in (23cm) length of ribbon and stitch one side of it to the left edge. Fold over to enclose the raw edges and slip stitch to secure.*

4 *Cut a second 9in (23cm) length of ribbon and, using a zipper foot, attach to one side of the zip (zipper). Stitch the ribbon edge to the other side of the zip.*

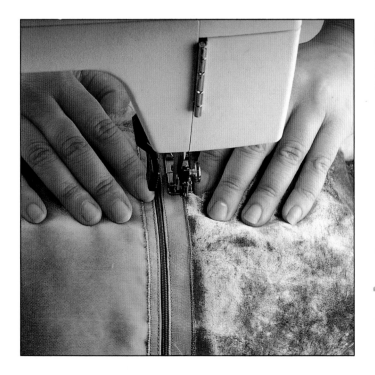

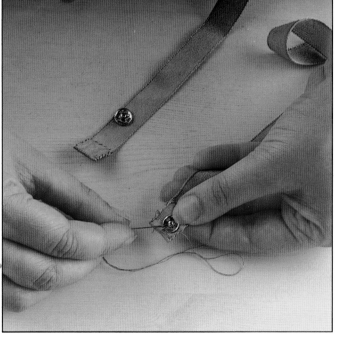

5 *Turn under the seam allowance along the edge of the lining velvet, then stitch the upper edge of the ribbon to the lining.*

6 *Make the strap from two pieces of ribbon, 8in (20cm) and 4in (10cm) long. Turn under one end of each piece enclosing the raw edges and securing with tiny slip stitches. Attach press studs (snaps) to the neatened ends and pin the raw ends to the lining ¼in (6mm) from the zip, and join the press studs together in the middle.* ▶

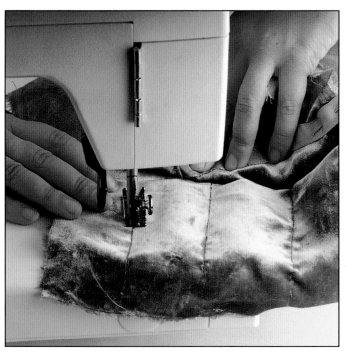

7 *Make the pocket section by folding the right side of the overlapping lining inwards and then turning it back on itself. Adjust until the pockets are 3in (7.5cm) deep.*

8 *Stitching lengthways, divide the fold up into four separate pockets, sewing through the layers of the lining only.*

9 *Turn under the raw edges on the right side and oversew (overcast) the lining to the outer fabric, to enclose the edges. Bind the top and bottom sides with ribbon as shown in Step 3. Machine-stitch one edge and catch down the other selvage with slip stitch. Tuck the ends in and oversew.*

10 *Make ties from two or four pieces of ribbon 10in (25cm) long. Turn under one raw edge on each piece and oversew two to the roll as shown above, or four as shown in the main picture. Trim the loose ends into a 'V' shape.*

Lavender Wreath

*L*avender is an important plant in the traditional cottage garden and has been widely cultivated over centuries for the perfume of its purple flowers. Its healing powers are used in aromatherapy to ease headaches and stress, and this wreath will fill any room in which it hangs with the rich scent of summer. The florist's technique of spiral-binding is used to attach the lavender stalks to a ready-made foundation wreath.

1 *Tie one end of the natural rope securely to the wreath.*

2 *Take a bunch of lavender and with one hand, hold it across the wreath with the flowers pointing outwards. Hold the rope in the other hand and wind it around the stalks, then over the wreath and spiral-bind the stalks in place.*

Materials:

natural sea grass rope or coarse string

ready-made twig wreath 12in (30cm) in diameter

dried lavender sprigs

3 *Place a second bunch of lavender to the right of the first bunch, and bind in place, wrapping the rope once or twice around the stalks to secure them in place. The next bunch goes to the right of the second, with the flowers pointing away from the wreath.*

4 *Continue to spiral-bind small bunches in the same way, making sure that the twig wreath is concealed. When the ring is completely covered, tie off the end of the rope securely and finish off with a loop for hanging.*

H a t p i n s

$\mathcal{A}$ selection of ornate hatpins was once an indispensable fashion accessory. A Victorian or Edwardian lady would seldom venture outdoors without wearing a hat, which would be held in place with several pins, fixed through her hair. These contemporary versions are made by threading beads to a specially-made pin, and may be used to decorate lapels, or hold scarves in place as well as adorn hats.

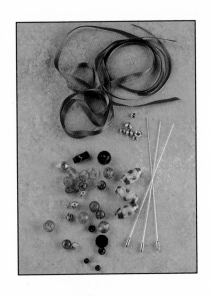

Materials:

decorative and diamanté beads

hatpin bases with safety ends

glue gun or impact adhesive

lengths of ¼in (6mm) wide ribbon in
several colours

matching sewing thread

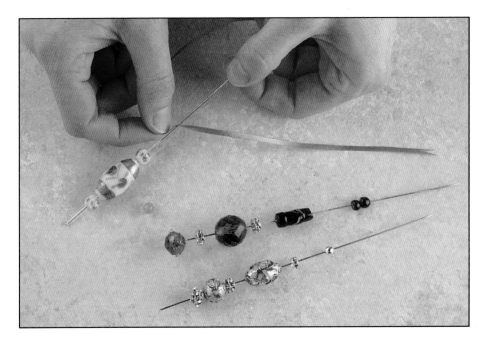

1 Choose a selection of beads in matching or complementary colours and in various shapes and sizes. Pick out a small bead to put on to the pin first to prevent the others slipping off. Smear the shaft of the pin with a very thin coat of glue, then add on the other beads.

2 Streamers can be added by threading a length of narrow ribbon between the beads. Tie into a bow and secure with a few stitches.

3 Make tiny roses from the ribbons, following the instructions on page 26. Sew the ends firmly and trim, before gluing the roses between the beads for a flowered effect.

Pincushion

$\mathcal{H}$eavily beaded pincushions are a typical example of the Victorian love of home decoration. They were often made by sailors as love tokens for their sweethearts, and would be adorned with anchors, flags, flowers and hearts. This pink taffeta cushion is stuffed with bran in the traditional way. Sawdust was also originally used, although a modern alternative filling could be substituted.

Materials:

6 x 12in (15 x 30cm) taffeta

matching sewing thread

bran or sawdust, to fill

rocaille embroidery beads in gold, pink and green

4 x ⅜in (1cm) pink crystal beads

⅛in (3mm) clear green glass beads

velvet in 2 contrasting colours

brass pins

an assortment of glass beads in different colours and sizes

sequins

5 rose-shaped buttons

1 Cut two 5in (12cm) squares of taffeta and sew together with a ⅜in (1cm) seam allowance, leaving a 1½in (4cm) opening at one side. Trim the corners, turn inside out and stuff, packing the filling in tightly. Slip stitch the gap to close. Thread a fine needle with a double length of thread.

2 Secure the thread to one corner of the cushion. Thread 15 gold rocaille beads on to the needle, then 2 pink, 1 green, 2 more pink, then 15 more gold. Insert the needle ⅜in (1cm) further along the outside edge, to make the first loop. Secure with two tiny overstitches, then make a second loop, passing the beads through the first loop before securing. Continue all around the cushion, adding a pink crystal bead to each of the corner loops.

3 Cover the edge of the cushion with a row of tiny clear green beads, threaded five at a time.

4 Cut out four hearts from velvet and put one, point outwards, on to the cushion as shown. Hold in place with pins, threaded with a small and a large bead. Outline each heart with different coloured beads.

70

5 *Cut out a diamond shape in velvet and place between the hearts in the centre of the cushion. Pin down each corner, threading a small bead and a sequin on first, then pin sequins along each of the four sides.*

6 *Attach a rose-shaped button to each corner and to the centre of the cushion. Ribbon roses could be used as an alternative (see page 26 for instructions).*

H a n d   T o w e l   a n d   W a s h c l o t h

*T*ransform a plain white hand towel and washcloth into an individual gift set, by adding appliquéd pansies in velvet and cotton prints. The pair would make a thoughtful and welcoming addition to a guest bathroom. The towel and washcloth should be able to stand up to normal wear and tear, so make sure that the fabrics used are colourfast, and wash them before sewing to avoid any shrinkage.

Materials:

8 x 6in (20 x 15cm) velvet

medium-weight washable iron-on interfacing

3 different cotton print fabrics

matching sewing thread

matching embroidery threads

white cotton hand towel and washcloth

1 *For the pansy appliqués, trace both parts of the two pansy templates on page 151. Back the piece of velvet with iron-on interfacing. Draw round the template on to the interfacing and cut out three large and one small inner petal shape from the interfacing-backed velvet. Cut one large flower shape from each of the three floral prints, and one small flower from one of them.*

2 *Pin and tack (baste) all the inner shapes to the flowers. Using a thread to match the velvet, satin stitch, by hand or machine, around the edge of the inner petals.*

3 *Embroider details on to the flowers with embroidery thread. Fill in the centre of each pansy with satin stitch, and sew the petal markings with two lines of stem or back stitch. Iron the interfacing to the back of each flower.*

4 Pin and tack the flowers to the corners of the towel and washcloth. Using a thread to match the flowers on the machine top and a white spool (bobbin) thread, appliqué in place. ◄

5 Cover the pile-free borders of the towel and washcloth with strips of floral cotton. Cut a piece 1½in (4cm) wide to fit from the edge to the pansies. Add ½in (12mm) at each end for turning under. Press under the long edges so that the strip just fits within the woven area. Pin and tack in place, then zig-zag to finish, with the machine threaded as before. ►

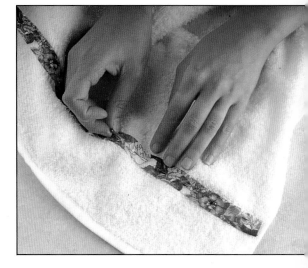

Bridal Gifts

A wedding is a unique celebration of love, and every bride will always treasure memories of her special day. The keepsakes in this chapter are perfect bridal gifts and are made using the finest materials: satins, lace, ribbons, silk flowers and pearls. Any one of them would delight a bride-to-be and all are sure to become cherished souvenirs.

Memories & Mementoes

A marriage is an occasion for great festivity among family and friends, and the ceremony itself has become the

focus for more customs and folklore than any other event. All over the world, and in all cultures,

time-honoured traditions are observed, as guests gather together to wish happiness to the bride and groom.

A wedding is a time when most people buy practical household items for the couple, perhaps choosing from a formal present list. But it can also be a wonderful opportunity to continue the tradition of making special romantic trousseau items for the bride-to-be.

The word trousseau literally translates as a "little bundle", and traditionally consisted of the clothes and linen that a bride had collected together to take to her new home. Over the years other people added extra gifts and accessories, from simple good luck tokens, such as decorative horseshoes or spoons, to luxurious garments, such as negligées, nightgowns and lingerie. A wedding shower, a party when the bride's close female friends give her their personal presents, is an American idea which is becoming increasingly popular elsewhere.

The bride's friends would sometimes join together to make her a commemorative quilt; in nineteenth-century America this was often an "album" quilt with each person contributing an individual block. Baltimore in particular became famous for its richly patterned patchwork and appli-

Above: Petals and fragrant strewing herbs were the forerunners of confetti. These were scattered across the path of a country bride as she approached the church. Rice, another symbol of fertility, was thrown after the newly married couple on their departure.

qué. A British wedding quilt of the same period, in contrast to these exuberant colours, consisted of a single sheet of plain fabric. The outline of the quilting design was transferred on to the cloth and the group of friends would then join in working the intricate, interlaced pattern.

The making of the wedding dress is surrounded by numerous superstitions. The groom must not see the dress until the actual service, and the final stitches should not be put in until just before the bride departs for the ceremony. Anybody who works on a wedding gown should hide a hair or a small coin inside the hem, and it is said that whoever sews the first stitch will herself be married within the year.

WEDDING TRADITIONS

The convention of a white wedding is comparatively recent; until the nineteenth century, a woman would be married in her favourite dress or a simple blue gown, a colour associated with purity and fidelity. During the American Revolution some republican women wore red as a symbol of defiance, while Icelandic brides wore black velvet embroidered with gold and silver.

The tradition of wearing blue is often continued as part of the custom of having "something old, something new, something borrowed and something blue" either on the dress, or as part of the bride's accessories. The "old" symbolizes the past, the

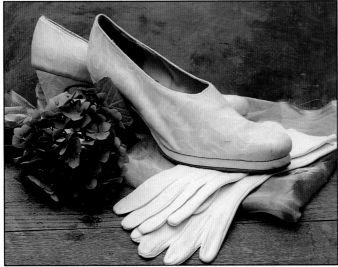

Above: The traditional white net veil is often a family heirloom and may be held in place with a coronet or garland of fresh flowers to match the bouquet. The veil covers the bride's face during the ceremony and is thrown back as she leaves church.

Above: Gloves were a favourite trousseau gift, to be worn or carried by the bride on her wedding day. Fine white kid leather was a popular choice for bridal gloves.

Right: Dried rosebuds have been threaded onto soft wire and formed into a heart to make this delicate love token, suitable for a bride or her bridesmaids.

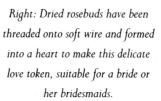

"new" looks to the future and the "borrowed" is a link with the present time. This tradition can be incorporated into a wedding gift by combining old lace, new ribbons and beads borrowed from a friend, along with an initial or small motif embroidered in blue.

The modern carnation boutonnières worn by the groom, best man, ushers and other guests, replace the bunch of ribbons, again often blue, that once would have decorated their hats. Both these favours are symbolic of the bonds of affection, or lover's knot, that will keep the couple together. The bride's lucky garter, still often worn today and sometimes thrown to the male guests after the service, shares the same origins. Stockings were once held up by ribbons and on her wedding day, a sixteenth-century bride would choose specially colourful ties which, after the solemn church ceremony, would be seized upon by the groom's friends, amid much uproar.

The exchanging of rings is a key point of the ceremony and in Britain they are usually entrusted to the best man. In the USA a young ring bearer is often chosen to carry the rings on a decorative cushion.

In the past, most brides carried wired cascades of flowers, but a more informal arrangement is now more common, sometimes decorated with ribbons and a lace frill. Brides are encouraged by their guests to fling their bouquets into the assembled party; tradition dictates that whoever catches it will be the next to marry. The choice of flowers is significant and usually

includes traditional favourites such as white roses, gypsophila (baby's breath), lily of the valley or orange blossom. When Queen Victoria married Prince Albert in 1840 she carried myrtle in her bouquet, a German tradition for bringing harmony to the household. Small favours in the form of sprigs of orange blossom, which represents fertility, tied with silver lace and satin ribbon, were handed to the distinguished guests as they arrived.

Wedding Anniversaries

first	cotton
second	paper
third	leather
fourth	silk
fifth	wood
sixth	iron
seventh	wool
eighth	bronze
ninth	pottery
tenth	tin
fifteenth	crystal
twentieth	china
twenty-fifth	silver
thirtieth	pearl
thirty-fifth	coral
fortieth	ruby
forty-fifth	sapphire
fiftieth	gold
fifty-fifth	emerald
sixtieth	diamond

TOKENS AND KEEPSAKES

The modern equivalents of these floral sprigs are almond favours, or bonbonnières, which originate from Italy, and add a decorative touch to the wedding reception. Five sugar almonds are bound up in layers of gauzy fabric to symbolize health, wealth, happiness, long life and fertility. The favours can form part of each guest's place-setting, or be arranged as a centrepiece and distributed at the end of the meal.

The reception provides an opportunity for the bride's and groom's relatives and friends to meet and to share in the couple's happiness. After the formal toasts, the main event is the cutting of the wedding cake, a tiered confection of icing, columns, cherubs, bells, horseshoes and flowers. The bride and groom usually cut the first slice from the cake together, but the top layer is often saved and stored away for the christening of their first child.

For those unable to attend the ceremony, a small portion of cake is often sent by mail in a specially bought box. For an unmarried girl, her share can have romantic significance. If a crumb is passed through a wedding ring, and then placed under her pillow, according to legend she will dream of her future husband.

Shoes are an unusual lucky symbol and tiny silver versions often decorate the cake. In Scotland a pair of baby shoes was tied on to the carriage as the couple departed for their honeymoon. Old boots or shoes are still thrown after the bride and groom as their guests cheer them on to their new life.

Above: Bonbonnières are easily made by cutting several circles of net or organza, placing the almonds in the centre and tying them round with ribbon. These examples are in the classic wedding colours of white, silver and blue.

Above: Victorian symbolism extended even to these ceramic cake supports. The female figure represents Ceres, goddess of the harvest and source of fertility; the ivy twining round the pillar stands for the ties of marriage, and the cupids are bringers of love and romance.

Above: The crescent shape of the horseshoe is an ancient symbol of growth and good luck. Along with cherubs, hearts and shoes, it has long been a favourite decoration for the wedding cake.

W e d d i n g S o u v e n i r B o x

*T*his gold-fringed box, topped by a trumpeting cherub, is the perfect hiding place for the photographs, letters, cards, invitations, cake decorations, preserved flowers and other ephemera that are bound to be collected as precious souvenirs of a special day. It is not complicated to put together and makes an imaginative gift for a bride-to-be, who would surely treasure it for many years.

1 *Cover the box and lid with white cartridge (drawing) paper and glue in place. The decorative paper used here is translucent, so any printing and labels on the shoebox will need to be hidden under a first layer of plain paper. If the wrapping paper chosen is opaque, this stage may be omitted.*

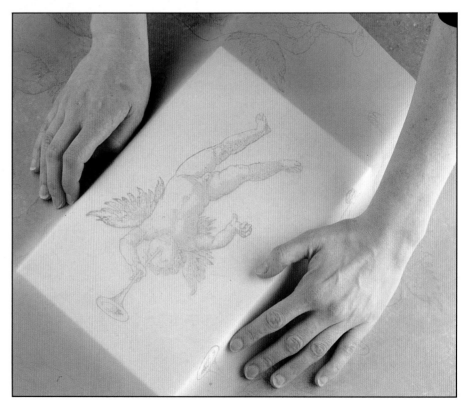

Materials:

shoebox

white cartridge (drawing) paper

PVA (white) glue

2 sheets wedding wrapping paper

1yd (1m) gold fringing

glue gun or contact adhesive

15 x 24in (38 x 60cm) taffeta

thin card (cardboard)

1yd x 1½in (1m x 4cm) white lace

2yd x 1in (1.8m x 2.5cm) gold ribbon

2 *Position the wrapping paper on the box lid to find the most attractive patterned area. Draw lightly around edge, add on the depth of the rim plus an extra margin of 1in (2.5cm) all round* and cut out. Glue to the lid using a thin layer of PVA (white) glue on the rim only, carefully mitring paper at the corners. Cover the rest of the box in the same way.

3 *Decorate the edges of the lid with the gold fringing, sticking it in place with a glue gun or contact adhesive.*

4 *Cut out a rectangle of taffeta for the lining 2in (5cm) wider than the box itself and 2in (5cm) longer than the base plus two sides. Fold under 1in (2.5cm) along the two side edges and glue into place inside the box. Cut two rectangles of thin card (cardboard) slightly smaller than the ends of the box. Cover with lining material and glue one at each end of the box, neatly tucking any surplus fabric underneath.*

5 *Trim the box with a border of white lace, attached to the inside rim with PVA glue and mitred at the corners. Tie the gold ribbon around the box, finishing off with a bow.*

W e d d i n g   Q u i l t

$\mathcal{T}$he intricate geometric pattern on this exquisite heirloom bed-spread features traditional marriage symbols: the true lover's knot, the wedding ring and the heart. The finished cover measures 2¼ft (2m) square but is made in four manageable sections, which are quilted separately before they are sewn together. For those daunted by the scale of this project, ask several friends and family members to help with the task by making a square each. The individual squares could be used to make smaller items such as a cushion, or even a pincushion.

Materials:

10yd x 45in (9m x 115cm) white cotton fabric

2¼ x 2¼ yd (2 x 2m) lightweight polyester wadding (batting)

white sewing thread

contrasting tacking (basting) thread

tissue paper

1 Cut eight squares of fabric, each 45in (115cm) square and four pieces of wadding (batting) 40in (100cm) square. Each quarter of the quilt is made in the following way. Assemble the backing fabric, wadding and top fabric together. Smooth out from the centre and pin. Measure 3in (7.5cm) border along two adjoining sides of the square and mark with tacking (basting) stitches. Tack the basic grid pattern of 6in (15cm) squares over the rest of the panel.

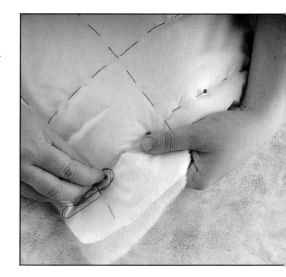

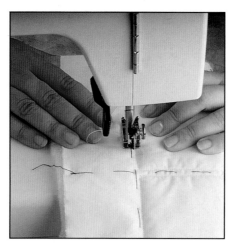

2 Machine-stitch two parallel lines, one either side of the tacking stitches.

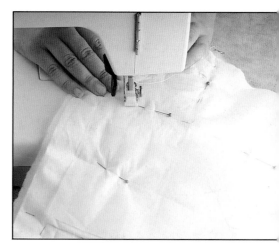

3 Trace the quilting design from pages 150–1 on to tissue paper leaving the 3in (7.5cm) border free on two adjoining sides of each and tack the tissue paper on to the reverse side of the square, within the grid lines, alternating the three designs to make a regular pattern. Lower the tread feed (feed dogs) and, using the darning foot, machine-stitch along the lines.

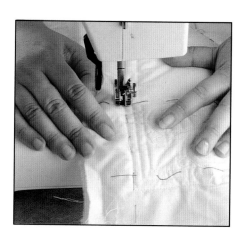

4 Trace the interlaced border design on page 150 and work in the same way. ◀

5 Join the four pieces by machine, stitching the top layers of cotton together. Trim the wadding, then join the underside layers by turning under the raw edges and oversewing (overcasting) together. Finish the outside edge by trimming back the wadding, turning in the raw edges and oversewing. ▶

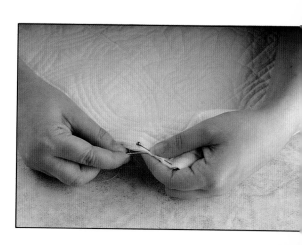

Initial Cushion

The bride's and groom's initials form the centrepiece of this delicate cushion. The letters, adapted from a sampler alphabet, are worked in embroidery silks and the cushion is edged with antique lace. A larger version could feature their names and even include the date and location of the wedding. The cushion can be made as a commemorative gift, or may be carried during the service by a ring bearer.

Materials:

6in square x 18 holes per inch (15cm square x 8 holes per cm) cream cross-stitch fabric (aida cloth)

stranded embroidery threads in different colours

6in (15cm) square cream silk backing fabric

matching sewing thread

polyester stuffing or kapok

1yd x 2½in (1m x 6cm) cream cotton lace

4 mother-of-pearl buttons

1 *Following the chart at the back of the book or using an alphabet of your own choice, embroider the initials on to the cross-stitch fabric. Work in cross stitch, using two strands of thread. Make sure that the four letters are squared up.*

3 *Join the ends of the lace together and run a gathering thread along the straight edge. Gather to fit around the outside of the cushion and pin in place, allowing for a little extra fullness at the corners. Oversew (overcast) the lace on to cushion with matching thread, using small, neat stitches. Finish off by sewing a mother-of-pearl button to each corner.*

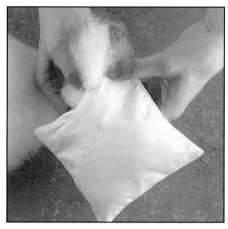

2 *Cut the backing fabric to the same size as the front piece of the cushion. Place the right sides together, pin and, allowing a ½in (12mm) seam, stitch together, leaving a 2in (5cm) gap at one edge. Trim the seam allowance and clip the corners, turn inside out and stuff firmly. Slip stitch the opening.*

Bride's Garter

The tradition of lucky wedding garters dates back many centuries. Elizabethan brides wore garters festooned with multi-coloured ribbons. This contemporary adaptation in alluring lace and satin would bring good fortune to any bride, as it incorporates elements that are old, new, borrowed and blue. The beaded frill is made from specially designed wedding lace which is decorated with bells and bows.

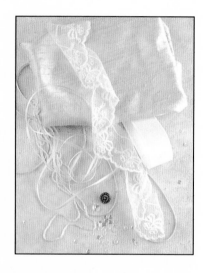

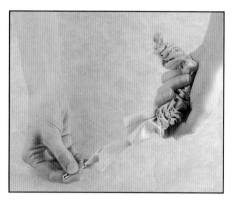

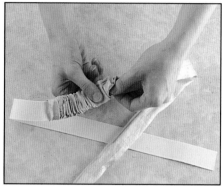

Materials:

4 x 36in (10 x 90cm) pale blue silk

matching sewing thread

safety pin

20 x 1¼in (50 x 3cm) elastic

1½yd x 2in (1.5m x 5cm) new lace

crystal rocaille embroidery beads

translucent blue and pearlized ¼in
(6mm) cup sequins

18 x ⅛in (45cm x 3mm) light blue
satin ribbon

12 x ¼in (30cm x 6mm) cream
satin ribbon

blue and cream sewing threads

old button (for luck)

1 *Sew together the long edges of the blue silk strip, leaving a ½in (12mm) seam allowance. Turn inside out by attaching a safety pin to one end and feeding it through the tube. Press lightly so that the seam lies at the back.*

2 *Fasten the safety pin to the elastic and draw the elastic through the silk tube. Stitch the ends firmly together. Turn the raw edges of the silk under and oversew (overcast) the edges of the tube together.*

3 *Cut two 24in (60cm) lengths of lace. Neatly join the ends of each piece to form a circle and decorate with beads and sequins, picking out the details of the pattern.*

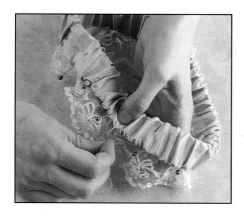

4 *Run a gathering thread along each straight edge of lace and draw up to the same diameter as the garter. Even out the fullness, pin, and oversew the lace on to the silk.*

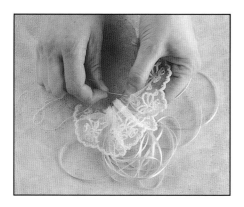

5 *Stitch the ends of the remaining piece of lace together. Gather tightly along the straight edge to form a rosette, and secure. Cut streamers of narrow blue and cream satin ribbon and sew on to the back of the rosette.*

6 *Sew the rosette on to the garter and finish by decorating with the old button for good luck.*

Heart Bag

An engraving in an old department-store catalogue provided the inspiration for this heart-shaped bag, which is just big enough to hold a lace handkerchief, lipstick and other essentials. It could be made as a present for the bride, in fabric to match her wedding gown, or as an accessory for each of the bridesmaids, to be carried with, or instead of, a posy. Whatever the purpose, it will make a wonderful memento.

Materials:

8 x 16in (20 x 40cm) heavy
interfacing

18 x 36in (45 x 90cm) cream silk

matching sewing thread

60 small seed pearls

60 small long pearl beads

13 x ³⁄₈in (1cm) pearl drop beads

2 large pearl drop beads

20 x 8in (50 x 20cm) mounting
board

PVA (white) glue

cream embroidery thread

12 x 18in (30 x 45cm) cream
lining silk

6 x 18in (15 x 45cm) striped silk

18 x 2in (45 x 5cm) cream lace

1yd x ¹⁄₈in (1m x 3mm) dark
cream ribbon

tapestry needle

1 Cut out two hearts from interfacing, to the size required. Cut two hearts from cream silk allowing an extra ³⁄₄in (18mm) all around. Tack (baste) the interfacing on to the silk hearts. Embroider one heart with pearls, using the photograph as a guide. Sew each bead on firmly, passing the thread twice through the fabric, but without pulling the backing fabric.

2 From mounting board, cut two rectangles 5 x 2in (12 x 5cm) for the side. From silk, cut two 7 x 4in (18 x 10cm) rectangles, to cover the sides. Place the board centrally on the silk and spread a thin layer of PVA (white) glue around the outer edges of the fabric. Fold over the corners, stretching the fabric slightly, then stick down the sides with extra glue where necessary.

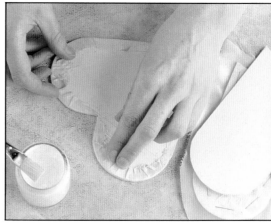

3 Cut two hearts from mounting board. Lay the beaded heart face-down and place one board heart on top, lining it up with the interfacing shape. Spread a thin layer of glue around the outside edge of the heart and gently stretch the surplus silk over it, easing the curves and clipping where necessary.

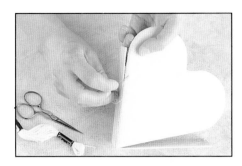

4 Using two strands of embroidery thread, whip stitch the two sides together along one short end, using small, neat stitches. Sew the front and back hearts on to the sides.

5 Join the lining fabric and striped silk along the long edge. With right sides together, join the side seam. Run a gathering seam along the lower open edge and draw up tightly so that excess fabric is on the wrong side.

6 Top stitch the length of lace to the striped fabric, then sew two parallel rows of straight stitch at the bottom edge of the lace to make a gathering channel. Position the lining inside the bag and pin in place. Sew the striped fabric to the top rim of the bag with small overstitching. Thread the ribbon through the channel with a large tapestry needle, and sew a large pearl drop bead to each end.

Good Luck Charm

*T*he gift of a wooden spoon is said to be a symbol of future domestic harmony, to be carried by the bride on her wedding day and then kept in her kitchen. As an alternative, a horseshoe can be similarly bound with cream silk and adorned with fabric flowers and pearls to make another lucky charm, which should always be hung with the open end facing upwards to prevent the good fortune from running out.

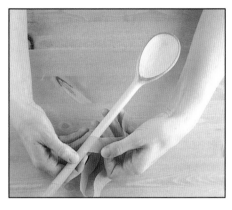

Materials:

wooden spoon

fine-grade sandpaper

white, gold and bronze
water-based paint

paintbrushes

16 x 1in (40 x 2.5cm) gold
gauze ribbon

cream sewing thread

28 x ⅜in (70cm x 1cm) cream
satin ribbon

16 x ⅜in (40cm x 1cm) pale
gold ribbon

28 x ¾in (70cm x 18mm) cream
satin ribbon

8 x ⅛in (20cm x 3mm) cream, pale
pink and dark gold ribbons

pink and cream fabric flowers

pearl beads

good luck token or charm

1 Smooth down any rough areas on the spoon with fine-grade sandpaper. Coat the bowl of the spoon with a light layer of white paint, allow to dry and colour wash with gold. Paint a narrow bronze line around the rim.

2 Secure the gold gauze ribbon to the top of the spoon with a few small stitches and bind it down the handle in a spiral. Finish off just above the bowl of the spoon with another stitch and neatly trim the end.

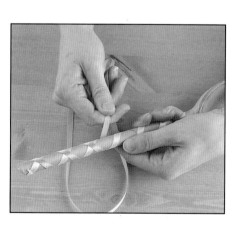

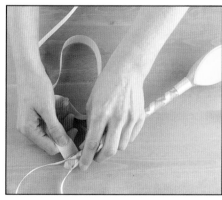

3 Fasten one end of the medium-width cream ribbon to the top of the spoon and bind down the handle, to cover the edges of the gold gauze. Secure and trim at the lower end, then bind the handle with medium-width gold ribbon in the same way, so that the spiral neatly crosses the cream ribbon.

4 Cut a 12in (30cm) length of medium-width cream ribbon and sew on to the top of the spoon to form a carrying loop. Cover the raw ends with 4in (10cm) lengths of wide cream ribbon.

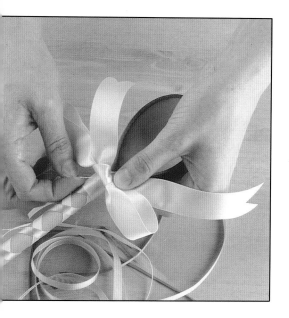

5 Tie a bow from the remaining cream satin ribbon and cut a "V" shape at each end to prevent it fraying. Sew the bow on to the spoon just above the bowl. Make streamers from folded lengths of the remaining ribbons and stitch on to the cream ribbon band.

6 Remove the plastic centres from the fabric flowers, and replace them with pearls. Sew the flowers all around the ribbon band, so that the spoon looks attractive from both front and back. Attach a special token or charm to the bow to bring extra good luck to the bride.

Christening Gifts

Every baby is special and should be welcomed into the world in style. Hand-sewn gifts provide a lasting token as a demonstration of the love and care that a new life deserves. The exquisite christening outfit on the following pages — comprising a full-length gown, bonnet and booties — will not only delight the friends and relatives who attend the christening, but will also be treasured as a family heirloom.

Newborn Celebrations

The birth of a new baby is a reaffirmation of life and a cause for celebration. The American custom of a "baby shower", which takes place prior to the child's arrival, is a charming idea. The mother's closest friends and family hold a party to share their knowledge of childbirth and motherhood, and to bring practical gifts that will be needed during the baby's first weeks.

In past centuries, giving birth was far more hazardous for both mother and child than it is today. Anxious parents would seek omens that might give possible indications as to their new child's future well-being, and various rituals and charms evolved. A baby born as the church bells rang out was believed to be endowed with special powers, and a baby's first bath had to be a soothing infusion of chamomile, lavender and rose petals. In Wales, a child was traditionally washed in rainwater to make it a good conversationalist. Simple presents, each with their own meaning, were donated to the family to bring good fortune to the child. These included salt, to give the child mental strength, matches to bring it light and guide its path, and bread, so that it would never go hungry.

The modern christening celebrates a child's name-giving and admittance into the church, but is also a recognition of its acceptance into the wider community. Similar ceremonial purification takes place in many cultures. In the ancient world, Hebrew, Egyptian and Greek infants all

Above: This christening outfit, in silk dupion, would be perfect for a winter baby. It has matching boots, bonnet and layers of petticoats and will be kept long after the event.

underwent ritual immersion as a symbol of spiritual cleansing. Today, the Jicarillo Indians of Mexico pour water from sacred rivers over the infant's head, while singing to it of the earth's riches.

During early Christian baptism a child was kept unclothed and would be fully submerged into a bath of flowing water. If it cried during this process it was seen as a good omen that would drive out any bad spirits. By the seventeenth century, holy water from the font was simply sprinkled over the baby's head and the child in its swaddling clothes would be carried in a simple linen wrap. The christening robe as we know it today evolved in the eighteenth century. It was made from white linen with a triangular yoke and a long gathered skirt with a matching close-fitting cap. Victorian babies were dressed in gowns decorated with Ayrshire work, a delicate form of white-on-white embroidery from the Scottish lowlands.

CHRISTENING GIFTS

A favourite nineteenth century idea which could be copied today is the layette pincushion. This was a small, cream satin cushion, edged with lace or a frill of the same fabric, and filled with bran or sawdust. Pins were pushed in to spell out messages and create patterns of flowers and leaves. "Welcome little stranger" or "Bless

Left: Lawn is the finest cotton fabric and because of its softness has always been used to make baby clothes. This christening dress has intricate embroidery and drawn-thread work, with ribbons to decorate the yoke.

Below: A lacy bib is a practical way to protect the christening gown from any mishaps, and can be made to match the dress itself.

Above: A necklace of coral beads was often a child's first present, a custom that dates back to Roman times. The silver bear napkin ring, made in 1910, was a christening gift for an Edwardian child.

the babe" were favourite greetings, and the date and place of birth were often included. More functional pincushions were also a popular gift. Until the invention of the safety pin in 1878, clothes were fastened with straight pins. To prevent injury, some mothers would actually sew their infants into their day clothes each morning. In Scotland the baby's shawl was held together with the luckenbooth – a silver heart-and-crown brooch. They were given as betrothal gifts and were pinned on to the children's shawls as a reminder of their parents' love.

Above: A basket represents the wealth and riches of the maternal body when given to a new mother and, like the pincushion, is a traditional and useful present. It can later be used to keep baby-care items or sewing equipment.

Coral has long been thought to have magic powers, and thick stems of it were used to make the handles of elaborate silver rattles. These were hung with tiny silver bells, whose sound both entertained the baby and warned away bad spirits. The Romans would hang a string of coral beads on the cradle to "preserve and fasten the

teeth", and it was also believed to protect against lightning and shipwrecks.

Wrapping a newborn baby in its mother's smock was once thought to endow that child with her charm and appeal, whilst in Ireland a child's first garment was the father's shirt. It was hoped that this would protect it from fairies who were always on the lookout for healthy babies to swap for their changelings. These folklore superstitions are echoed in the christening quilt on page 106, which uses a combination of old shirting and dress prints. The patchwork is based on the four-patch block, the first pattern that was taught to children, and it is very easy to assemble by hand or machine. The design is also known as "beggar-my-neighbour", since extra scraps of cloth would have to be cajoled from family and acquaintances.

Nineteenth century christenings were grand occasions, with all the guests dressed in their finest clothes and the baby in a blue fur-trimmed mantle. Royal christenings, when the infant princes and princesses wore the finest lace and silk, were the most formal of all. This did not prevent the mood being shattered at Queen Victoria's baptism in June 1819 by her godfather, the Prince Regent, who was in a bad temper. As the priest announced each of her names he shouted out his objections, to the accompaniment of her mother's sobs. She had wanted her daughter to be called Georgiana Charlotte Augusta, but the name finally settled upon was Alexandrina Victoria.

The role of the godparents, undertaken at the child's baptism, is to give spiritual guidance throughout its life. Christening presents from godparents have special significance and are often made from silver; perhaps a spoon or mug for a boy and a bracelet or other jewellery for a girl.

When choosing or making a gift for a newborn baby, a good source of colours and motifs can be found in the traditional lists of birthstones and plants. The plants can vary among countries, but are always flowers that bloom during the birthday month. This list comes from nineteenth-century America.

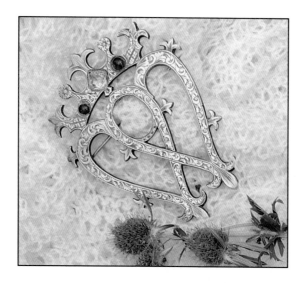

Left: This double-heart luckenbooth is made from engraved silver and is inlaid with paste gems. It rests on a finely knitted Shetland shawl, made from single-ply wool, itself a time-honoured baby gift.

Left: A baby album can be compiled to record a child's developments and achievements in its first years, and can also include other images from childhood, such as decorative scraps.

Birthstones and Plants

Month	Gemstone	Flower
January	*garnet*	*snowdrop*
February	*amethyst*	*primrose*
March	*jasper*	*violet*
April	*sapphire*	*daisy*
May	*emerald*	*hawthorn*
June	*agate*	*honeysuckle*
July	*turquoise*	*water lily*
August	*carnelian*	*poppy*
September	*chrysolite*	*morning glory*
October	*beryl*	*hops*
November	*topaz*	*chrysanthemum*
December	*ruby*	*holly*

Christening Gown

Traditionally, a christening gown is passed down through the family and the same dress can be traced through successive generations of photograph albums, worn by boys and girls alike. This classic robe is made from cotton lawn and features a lace-trimmed collar and centre panel. Along with its matching bonnet and brocade shoes, it makes an outfit that will be handed on as a family heirloom.

1 *Cut out all the pattern pieces on pages 144–5, enlarging to the size required. All seam allowances are ⅝in (1.5cm) and are finished by zig-zagging close to the stitching and trimming. Stitch the right-hand shoulder seam of the collar to the matching seam on the collar facing. Trim the seam allowance to ⅛in (3mm) and press open. With right sides together, sew round three sides of the collar leaving it open along the front neck edge. Trim seams, clip corners, turn through the opening and press.*

Materials:

2¼yd x 45in (2m x 115cm) cream lawn (fine cotton)

matching sewing thread

5yd x ¾in (4.6m x 18mm) cotton lace

18in (45cm) narrow elastic

press stud (snap)

hook and eye

2 mother-of-pearl buttons

seed pearl beads

2 *Following the markings on the pattern pieces, pin, tack (baste) and stitch the lace in position on the collar and the centre front panel of the skirt, mitring the angles.*

3 Sew the shoulder seams of the yoke and the yoke facing, trim the seam allowance to ⅛in (3mm) and press open. Press up the seam allowance along the front and back edge of the yoke facing. ◀

4 Sew the front side panels to the centre lace-trimmed panel. Join the back seam as far as the large dot shown on the pattern. Neaten the edge of the facing, fold to the inside and tack along the top edge. Gather between the notches on the front and back. With right sides together, pin the front and back to the yoke. Adjust the gathers, tack and stitch. Press gathering towards the yoke and trim. ▲

5 Pin and tack the collar to front neck edge of the yoke. Pin and tack the yoke facing to the yoke with right sides together. ▲

6 Stitch up the centre back and round the neck edge. Trim and clip curves before turning right-side out. Press the yoke facing to the inside. Pin, then slip stitch along the bottom edge. ▶

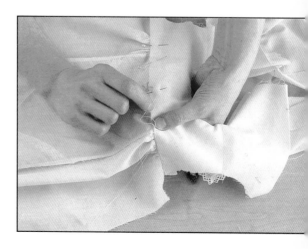

7 Turn up ⅛in (3mm) along the bottom edge of the sleeve and machine stitch. Trim and turn up again. Pin and tack the lace on the right side and straight stitch in position. ▲

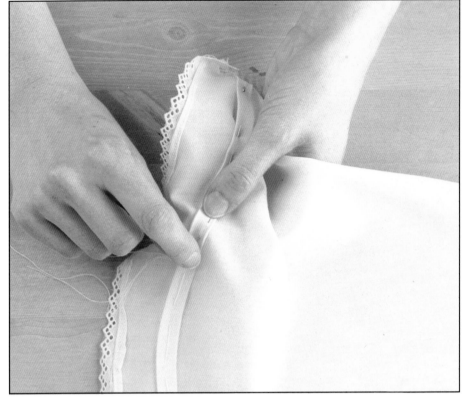

8 Cut out and sew a 12in (30cm) bias strip of lawn on the inside of the sleeve as shown. Thread elastic through this casing and adjust to fit. Sew securely in place at each end. ▶

9 Gather the sleeve head between the notches. Pin and tack into the armhole, adjusting the gathers. Straight stitch the seam, then zig-zag and trim as before. Sew the sleeve and side seams. Finish the hem with a lace border as described in Step 7 for the sleeves. ◀

10 Sew a press stud (snap) to the neck edge of the collar and a hook and eye at the shoulder edge. Make two button holes in the right back yoke and sew the buttons on the left side. Trim the lace collar with seed pearl beads. ▼

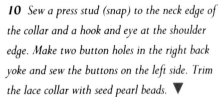

Christening Bonnet

This appealing baby bonnet is made from the softest cream lawn (fine cotton) to co-ordinate with the christening gown. It could also be made on its own, perhaps in a floral print fabric, to form part of a layette. The peak is finished with a simple cotton lace, then folded back to frame the baby's face. A rouleau tie fastens under the chin, held in place by tiny broderie anglaise rosettes with seed pearl centres.

Materials:

12 x 36in (30 x 90cm) cream lawn
(fine cotton)

matching sewing thread

12in (30cm) narrow elastic

20 x ¾in (50 x 18mm) cotton lace

safety pin

seed pearl beads

1 Following the pattern on page 146, and enlarging to the size required, cut out two crowns from cream lawn (fine cotton). Sew together along the straight edge, then stay stitch around the seam allowance on one piece, trimming and notching to the stitch line. Cut out the two bonnet pieces from cream lawn.

2 Using a pencil, lightly transfer the dots from the pattern to the bonnet pieces. Allowing a seam of ½in (12mm), sew the pieces together around the sides and peak, leaving the back edge open. Trim edges and clip corners, turn inside out and press. Gather the back edge between dots. Pin and tack (baste) to the crown, matching up the dots and adjusting the gathers before sewing. Press towards the crown then trim and notch the curved edge.

3 Pin and tack the crown facing on to the inside of the main bonnet. Straight stitch through all layers ¼in (6mm) from the straight edge of the crown. Thread elastic through this channel. Sew one end securely, adjust to fit and fasten the other end before trimming. Hem the facing.

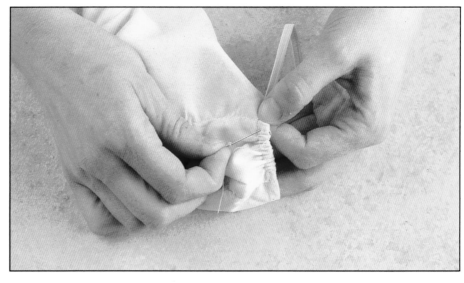

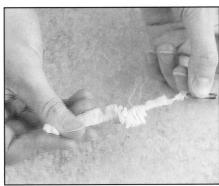

4 *Pin and tack the lace to the underside of the front edge, mitring the corner. Tuck the ends under and stitch.*

5 *Make the rouleau tie from a 16 x ¾in (40cm x 18mm) wide bias strip of lawn, joining several pieces if necessary. Fold in half and stitch long sides together ¼in (6mm) from the folded edge. Fasten a small safety pin to one end and draw the tube inside out. Press lightly and stitch securely to each end of the lace trim.*

6 *Make two small rosettes from the remaining lace by running a gathering thread along one edge and drawing up. Decorate with a cluster of seed pearl beads. Sew on to the bonnet over the rouleau joins.*

Christening Booties

*M*others have always valued their baby's first pair of shoes as a keepsake, and these sumptuous brocade booties would be worth cherishing! Lined with silk and decorated with a fine organza frill and a golden tassel, they would be worthy of any fairytale prince or princess. The same basic pattern is used for the broderie anglaise variation, which has a lace-edged heart decorating the toe.

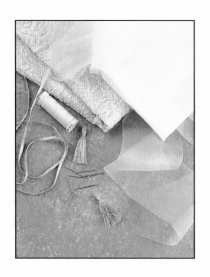

Materials:

9 x 36in (23 x 90cm) brocade

9 x 36in (23 x 90cm) lining

24 x ⅛in (60cm x 3mm) gold ribbon

24 x 3in (60 x 7.5cm) sheer ribbon

matching sewing thread

2 small gold tassels

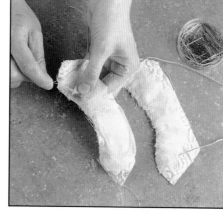

1 *Following the pattern on page 146, and enlarging to the size required, cut two sides, two fronts and two soles from brocade and lining fabrics. Snip the notches and transfer all markings. Cut the gold ribbon into four equal lengths and tack (baste) to the right side of the brocade bootie sides at the crosses. Cut the sheer ribbon in half, fold each half lengthways and pin the long edges together. Cut the ends in a curve.*

2 *Gather the long edges of the ribbon and pin to the right side of the brocade bootie sides between the crosses. Pull up the gathers to fit and tack in place.*

3 *Pin the lining and brocade sides together with the right sides facing. Stitch together along the upper curved edges, taking a ¼in (6mm) seam allowance. Snip the seam allowance around the curves and turn to the right side. Press lightly, then tack the raw edges together.*

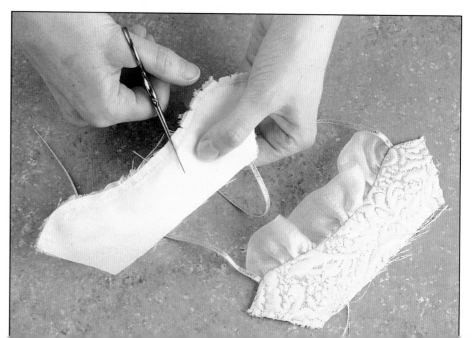

4 *Butt the front edges of the sides together, matching up the dots, and whip stitch together. With right sides facing, pin the brocade front to the top of the bootie and the lining front to the underside, matching the dots. Stitch the front seam. Tack the raw edges of the fronts together with the wrong sides facing.*

5 *Turn the bootie through to the wrong side. With right sides facing, pin then tack the brocade sole to the bootie matching up the notches. Stitch, taking a ¼in (6mm) seam allowance. Pin and tack the lining sole to the bootie in the same way, sandwiching the upper part between the soles.*

6 *Stitch, leaving a 2in (5cm) gap along a straight edge. Snip the curved edge of the soles, then turn the upper part through to the wrong side. Turn under the raw edge of the lining and slip stitch the seam closed. Turn to the right side and sew a small gold tassel securely to the front of the bootie.*

Christening Quilt

Welcome a new baby into the family circle with this irresistable patchwork quilt. It is made from a harmonious mixture of old and new fabrics, which can be bought or begged from friends and relations. By using both pink and blue shades it will, according to custom, be suitable for either a girl or boy. It is essential that only lightweight flameproof wadding (batting) is used for the filling.

Materials:

assortment of striped shirting and floral fabrics of similar weight

2in (5cm) square template cut from thin card (cardboard)

matching sewing thread

1yd (1m) square backing fabric

1yd (1m) square lightweight polyester wadding (batting)

quilting thread (if quilting by hand)

64 mother-of-pearl buttons (optional)

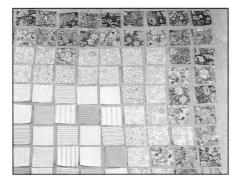

1 Wash all the fabric pieces and press. Using the photograph as a guide, cut out squares along the grain of the fabric. The quilt as shown uses 225 in shirting, 136 in light floral fabrics and 168 in dark floral fabrics. Lay out the shirting squares in 15 rows of 15 squares, so that the stripes form a basket-weave pattern. Border with two rows each of light and dark floral squares.

2 Join the squares by hand or machine in units of four leaving a ⅜in (1cm) seam. Press the seams open and pin each block of four with right sides together, matching up the corners. Sew the blocks together, until the top layer is completed.

3 Cut the backing fabric and wadding (batting) to the same size as the quilt plus 2in (5cm) all round. Sandwich the three layers together, with the wadding in the middle with outer fabrics right-side out. Smooth out the layers and pin together. Tack (baste) all the seams.

4 Quilt by hand or machine, following the seam lines exactly. Sew the first and last two rows two squares in from the edge, and leave three squares between the centre lines of stitching.

5 *Join 2in (5cm) strips of one of the dark floral fabrics to fit all around the outside of the quilt. Press ½in (12mm) under along one long edge. With right sides together and raw edge of the strip along the edge of the quilt, sew the binding on to the quilt, ½in (12mm) from the edge, mitring the corners. Slip stitch the neatened edge to the backing fabric to enclose the raw edges.*

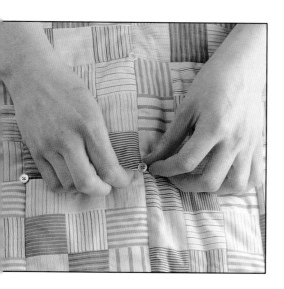

6 *If desired, sew on mother-of-pearl buttons at the points where the quilting lines intersect, making sure that they are attached very firmly so that they cannot be pulled off by the child.*

Sweet Nothings

Friends and family have always exchanged presents with special meaning, whether Valentines, homemade preserves, pot plants or the ubiquitous bunch of flowers. The keepsakes on the following pages are perhaps the most romantic gifts of all — these "sweet nothings" are charming symbols of love and affection, made from lavish silks, velvets, organza and lace, lavender and roses.

H e a r t - f e l t   G i f t s

"The greatest pleasure of life is love; the greatest treasure, contentment; the greatest possession, health; the greatest ease, sleep and the best medicine, a true friend." This sentimental inscription comes from a scrapbook compiled in the nineteenth century, a time when many women kept a "friendship album" as a record of their lives and the people they knew. Family and acquaintances would be invited to write messages, paint, draw or make some other small memento, which was then pasted into the album, alongside a random collection of engravings, invitations and other ephemera.

*P*rinted scraps were especially popular, and the newly developed chromolithography process meant that brightly coloured sheets of embossed images could be printed quickly and cheaply. Every conceivable subject was illustrated: nursery rhymes, royalty, animals and birds, children, cherubs, soldiers and sailors, all kinds of flowers and fashionable women, new inventions and buildings – even steam trains and the Eiffel Tower.

Scraps are most usually associated with Valentine cards. The celebration of St Valentine's Day as 14 February – a time for universal declarations of friendship and adoration – was originally a European tradition which spread to America at the height of its popularity in the nineteenth century. Lupercalia, the Roman festival of youth, took place in mid-February, and it was also believed to be the time when birds picked their mates for the year ahead and began to build their nests. The Christian church, in an effort to secularize the sometimes rowdy

Above: A single red rose is still recognized as a declaration of love – this charmingly simple flower in its old handmade terracotta pot would be a delightful present for Valentine's Day.

festivities, allocated the day its own patron saint, the obscure martyr St Valentine.

LOVE TOKENS

Many superstitions and customs grew up around Valentine's Day. It was said that a

girl could dream of her future husband by placing bay leaves under her pillow before going to sleep the night before, and that the first unattached member of the opposite sex seen the next day would become her Valentine. In villages, lots were drawn to allocate potential suitors, and gifts and cards were swapped.

Cards were not sent only to lovers, however, but were also exchanged between friends and relatives. Originally they were seen as a serious declaration of love or proposal of marriage, but later became simply tokens of friendship. They developed into elaborate multi-layered confections of tinsel, beads, feathers, scented pads, paper lace, and scraps featuring cupids, hearts and flowers. Sometimes they were sent anonymously but the name or initials of the anxious sender were usually concealed under a tab or pull-out flap.

The manufacture of Valentine cards became a thriving business; they were assembled in large workshops and sold through

stationery shops. The new British postal system of 1840 – the penny post – and the rapidly expanding railway network meant that cards could for the first time be cheaply sent all over the country. Public enthusiasm was so great that London postmen in the mid-century were so busy on 14 February that they demanded extra meal allowances in return for their heavy workload. On the other side of the Atlantic, in Worcester, Massachusetts, the enterprising Esther Howland set up a card-making business specializing in collages, which achieved an annual turnover of $100,000 and made her fortune.

The wording of Valentine cards has not changed greatly over the years – traditional

Above: The muted, nostalgic colours of dried and everlasting flowers, pot-pourri and pressed flowers are reminders of long summer days.

Above: a heart pierced by Cupid's arrow is one of the most enduring of romantic motifs, and occurs throughout the history of art and applied design.

messages such as "when this you see, remember me"; "kiss me quick and love me forever"; "a gift of love"; "forget me not"; "offering of friendship" – could still today be embroidered on cushions or samplers, or adapted to some other keepsake.

The images were equally romantic, and included cherubs bearing garlands of flowers, hearts, pairs of doves, lovebirds, roses and clasped hands. These motifs of love and friendship contained a secret language which added an extra significance; some were easily interpreted, but others were more obscure. The heart is a universal symbol, recognized as "the source of love and the centre of the soul", so any heart-shaped gifts have special meaning. Hands clasped together mean "hands in trust forever", or when holding a heart symbolize "undying bonds of friendship". The latter motif appears on the *Claddagh*, the Irish betrothal ring. The beaded hearts on page 128 are a good way to use old treasured scraps of lace; a fabric which has always been much treasured and was in the past worn as a symbol of wealth.

THE LANGUAGE OF FLOWERS

Flowers have always been highly valued as symbols of friendship and an elaborate code has grown up around them, a language of flowers. This idea appealed greatly to Victorian sentiment, but appeared long before the nineteenth century. Shakespeare wrote of rosemary symbolizing remembrance and pansies for thoughts. In the 1740s, Lady Mary Wortley Montagu sent an excited letter to her sister: "There is no flower that has not a verse belonging to it; and you may quarrel, reproach or send letters of passion or friendship without even inking your fingers." Dictionaries of flower meanings were published and eagerly studied; at a time when courtship was either clandestine or chaperoned, the language of flowers could be used to send messages of love. The attributes were directly linked to the characteristics of the plant – everlasting flowers meant "always remembered" and the scarlet poppy "fantastic extravagance". The narcissus stood for "egotism and self-love" after the ancient myth. There would be no doubting the intent of somebody who sent a bunch of tuberose, which translated as "I

An Alphabet of Plants and Flowers

apple	*temptation*
buttercup	*golden riches*
cabbage	*profit*
daisy	*beauty and innocence*
elm	*dignity*
forget-me-not	*true love*
garden sage	*esteem*
honeysuckle	*bonds of love*
ivy	*wedded love, fidelity*
jonquil	*I desire a return of affection*
king cup	*I wish I was rich*
lily of the valley	*return of happiness*
michaelmas daisy	*cheerfulness in old age*
nettle	*slander*
olive	*peace*
primrose	*I have confidence in you*
queen's rocket	*the queen of coquettes*
rosebud, white	*too young to love*
sunflower	*lofty and pure thoughts*
tulip, variegated	*beautiful eyes*
ulex (gorse)	*anger*
venus fly trap	*deceit*
weeping willow	*melancholy, forsaken lover*
xanthium	*rudeness*
yew	*sorrow*
zinnia	*thoughts of absent friends*

have seen a lovely girl". A mixed bouquet could spell out a more complicated message such as "let the bonds of love unite us", consisting of blue convolvulus (the bonds), ivy (marriage), and straws (unite).

Attempts have always been made to preserve the heady scents of summer flowers and the myriad colours of petals to enliven the dreary winter months. This was once a matter of necessity, as much as decoration, for dried flowers and fresh herbs were used to disguise the odours that lingered around the house. Nosegays and posies were carried in the street to mask bad smells; and indoors, rooms were scented with flowers and pungent oils.

Large porcelain jars with perforated lids were made to contain moist pot-pourri. Fresh petals were packed down in layers with spices and fixatives, gradually fermenting over time. Dry pot-pourri is now more common and can be made easily. There are numerous recipes, but the main constituent is usually dried rose petals, picked when the flowers are in full bloom. These are mixed together with smaller quantities of other ingredients: geranium leaves, lavender, verbena, bay and rosemary for their perfume, and marigold, delphinium and sunflower petals for colour. Orris root, sweet gums and spices can all be used to enhance and preserve the scents. Pot-pourri bags and sachets can be made using small remnants of floral cottons, but look especially attractive when made out of lace or translucent fabrics that do not conceal the colours of the petals.

Left: Citrus pomanders have a long-lasting spicy, wintry scent which makes them ideal as Christmas decorations. They are made by studding an orange, lemon or lime with cloves before rolling in orris root and ground spices, and allowing to dry out completely.

Below: This lacey valentine is a lasting reminder of affection. It is made from slubbed silk and trimmed with small bows and ribbon roses.

Above: Metallic organza and silver cord add an antique feel to these pot-pourri sachets. They can be kept in the lingerie drawer but are pretty enough to leave out. If they are placed near a radiator, the rising heat will diffuse the fragrance.

113

Pot-pourri Bags

*O*nly the most basic sewing techniques are required to make these delightful small bags. The round, pomander-shaped versions are made from circles of fabric edged with lace, and the sachets are simply stitched around three sides, filled with pot-pourri and tied up with ribbon bows. Several bags made in toning floral prints would look effective grouped together in a wicker basket.

Materials:

12in (30cm) square floral-printed cotton

matching sewing thread

1½yd x 2in (1.5m x 5cm) lace

pot-pourri

silk or velvet flowers and leaves

1yd x ⅛in (1m x 3mm) ribbon in each of 3 colours

1 *Draw around a dinner plate on to floral-printed cotton to make a circle, then cut it out.*

2 *Stitch the lace around the outside edge of the fabric and join the ends neatly together.*

3 *Run a gathering thread just below the bottom edge of the lace. Gather up the thread, and fill the bag with pot-pourri, then pull up the thread to leave a 1in (2.5cm) gap.*

4 *Sew the leaves and flowers around the inside edge of the bag, then pull up the gathering thread and tighten securely, making sure that all the flowers are fixed in place. Tie the ribbons below the lace, finishing off with a bow.*

Cornucopia

For Victorians, Christmas was a time of great celebration, and the focus of togetherness became the tree, newly popularized in the 1840s by the royal family. As now, children would adorn the branches with baubles, bows, candles, tinsel and toys. A cornucopia filled with bonbons, was a favourite decoration, which still makes an unusual container for a gift at any time of the year.

1 With the pair of compasses and ruler measure a quarter-circle on the card (cardboard) with a radius of 8in (20cm). Cut out and clip the end from the point. Cover with taffeta using PVA (white) glue, mitring the corners neatly.

2 Bend the card to make a cone, butting together the edges. Neatly whip stitch the fabric edges together, then glue on a strip of gold ribbon to cover the seam.

Materials:

pair of compasses

ruler

8in (20cm) square thin card (cardboard)

matching sewing thread

10in (25cm) square taffeta

PVA (white) glue

28 x 1/8in (70cm x 3mm) gold ribbon

24 x 1/2in (60cm x 12mm) gold braid

12 x 20in (30 x 50cm) printed organza

bodkin

12 x 1/2in (30cm x 12mm) gold lace

scrap of tasselled furnishing braid

3 Cut a 12in (30cm) length of gold braid to form the hanging loop. Glue to each side of the inside rim and leave to dry.

4 Sew the two short edges of the organza together and press the seam open. Fold in half with the seam on the inside and stay stitch the open edges together. Make a drawstring channel 1in (2.5cm) from the folded edge by sewing two rows of straight stitch 1/4in (5mm) apart. Run a gathering thread along the lower edge, gather to fit just inside the rim and glue in place.

5 *Thread the narrow gold ribbon through a bodkin and insert it through the drawstring channel, by pushing the point of the bodkin through the organza.* ◀

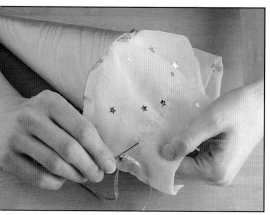

6 *Trim the rim of the cone with lengths of gold lace and braid, gluing them in place and neatening the overlap. Sew tiny tassels, cut from the furnishing braid, to the ends of the drawstring and to the point of the cone.* ▶

117

Scented Cushions

The cotton velvet for these cushions has been hand-dyed to obtain the soft, rich shades. This is a simple process, but store-bought colours are just as suitable, although they may not be as subtle. The cushions are perfumed with pot-pourri or by sprinkling perfume between the layers of wadding (batting), and appliquéd with nostalgic designs of clasped hands, hearts and doves carrying love letters.

1 Cut two 3 x 9in (7.5 x 23cm) pieces for the border in one colour, and a central panel of 5 x 9in (12 x 23cm) in a contrasting shade. With long sides together, join the two border stripes to either side of the central panel.

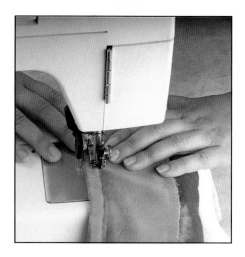

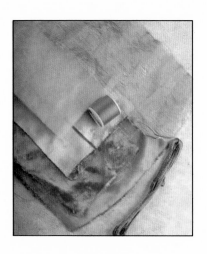

Materials:

14 x 36in (36 x 90cm) velvet

5 x 9in (12 x 23cm) contrasting velvet

5 x 9in (12 x 23cm) metallic organza

tissue paper

embroidery hoop

matching sewing thread

metallic thread

7 x 8in (20cm) squares of polyester wadding (batting)

pot-pourri or perfume

3 skeins stranded embroidery thread

thin card (cardboard)

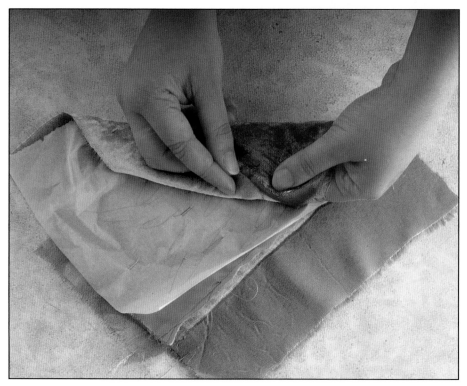

2 Pin and tack (baste) the organza to the right side of the central panel, squaring up the weave of the fabric. Trace your design on to a piece of tissue paper and tack to the back of the panel.

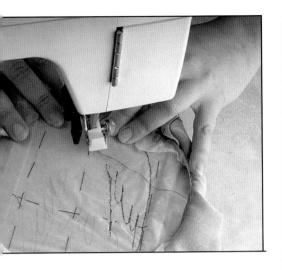

3 Stretch the piece out in an embroidery hoop and straight stitch over the design through both layers of fabric. ▲

4 Remove from the hoop, turn over and use a sharp pair of scissors to trim away the excess organza from the edges of the design. ▶

5 Put the piece back in the hoop, right side up. Thread the machine with metallic thread and sew a narrow zig-zag over the straight stitch to secure the raw edges. ◀

6 Cut two pieces of main colour velvet 7 x 9in (18 x 23cm) to form the back of the cushion. Turn under and stitch one long side on each piece. ▼ ▶

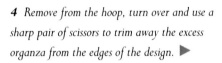

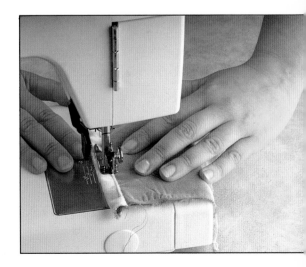

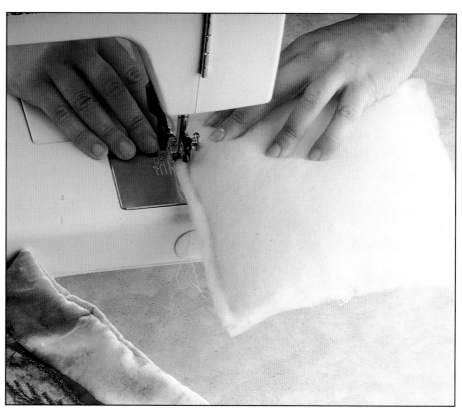

7 *With right sides together, pin the back pieces to the front, so that one piece overlaps the other. This will form the envelope-style closure. Sew around the outside of the square, leaving a ¹/₂in (12mm) seam all around, clip the corners and turn right sides out.* ▲

8 *Make the cushion pad by stacking the squares of wadding (batting) together, layering pot-pourri between them, or sprinkling with* perfume. Sew together through all the layers, close to the edge. Zig-zag to neaten the seam and trim. Place inside the cushion cover. ▲

9 *Make the tassels by winding the embroidery thread around a 2in (5cm) piece of card (cardboard). Sew the thread together along the top and cut at the bottom to release the tassel fringe.* ◀

10 *Bind the threads together ¹/₂in (12mm) from the top, leaving a length of thread with which to sew the tassel on to the cushion.* ▼

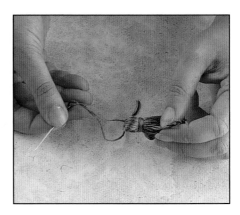

Rose and Lavender Posy

A bouquet always makes a welcome gift, but a bunch of carefully selected and beautifully arranged dried flowers will long outlast fresh blooms, to become an enduring reminder of a happy occasion. The "language of flowers" interprets the meaning of lavender as "devoted attention" and the pink rose as a symbol of affection, so this posy should really only be made for a very special friend.

Materials:

florist's wire

12 large artificial or glycerined leaves

florist's green tape

dried lavender stems

bunch of dried rosebuds

paper ribbon

1 *Fold a piece of florist's wire one-third of the way along its length, to form a 6in (15cm) stalk. Attach a leaf to the top by its stalk, and bind in place with florist's green tape, pulling and wrapping the tape down to the end of the wire. Repeat the process to make 12 leaves.*

2 *Divide the lavender into several small bunches. Hold them together loosely, setting the bunches at an angle to give a good shape. This will form the basic structure of the posy.*

3 *Taking a single rosebud at a time, push the stems into the lavender, spacing them out evenly.*

4 *If desired, bind the posy with florist's wire so it will keep its shape while you work. Then edge the posy with the wire-mounted leaves. Bind in place again.* ◄

5 *Unravel the paper ribbon and use to bind all the stalks together tightly, covering the wire and the stalks completely. Finish off by tying the ends of the ribbon into a bow.* ►

Valentine

*S*himmering layers of shot crystal organza, in delicate greens and golds, frame a luxuriant red velvet heart in this Valentine. The fabric is stitched down by machine in intricate patterns, using a combination of sewing cotton and metallic embroidery threads to produce a rich texture. It makes an enchanting love token, which anybody would be delighted to receive on 14 February.

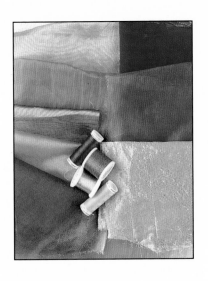

Materials:

assortment of organzas, including green and pink

8in (20cm) embroidery hoop

assortment of shot crystal and metallic organzas

sewing threads in burgundy and mint green

metallic machine-embroidery thread in gold and purple

scrap of dark red velvet

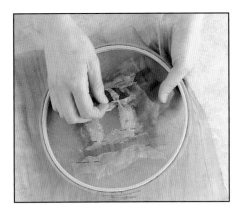

1 Stretch a piece of green organza into the embroidery hoop as the foundation fabric. Cut short narrow strips of different fabrics and pin down to build up the border. Cut a square of pink organza to go in the centre.

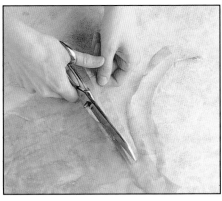

2 Cut three ½ x 12in (12mm x 30cm) lengths of metallic organza to outline the design. Use one piece of organza to define the centre square.

3 Twist the remaining two strips and pin them down in curls and zig-zags on either side of the centre. Machine-stitch down all the fabrics with gold thread outlines.

4 Cut out a heart from red velvet as the centrepiece and pin it in place. Add more colour and definition to the design by incorporating patterns embroidered in burgundy, metallic purple and mint threads. Embroider the heart into the centre. Once removed from the hoop, the Valentine can be left as it is, mounted in a card or small frame, or made into a tiny cushion.

Catch-all

$\mathcal{T}$his curious bag is based on a design that originally appeared in a Victorian craft manual. Its name reveals its purpose: a generally useful holder for anything from knitting wools or sewing, to letters, writing materials and notebooks. Made up in extravagant silks and brocade, a catch-all could be used as an exciting way to disguise a present or it could be given as a gift in itself.

Materials:

mounting (matting) board

stapler

6 x 22in (15 x 55cm) printed lining fabric

PVA (white) glue

12 x 20in (30 x 50cm) pink silk dupion

matching sewing thread

8 x ¹⁄₃in (8mm) brass curtain rings

1yd (1m) fine gold cord

12in x 1yd (30cm x 1m) gold silk dupion

1 tassel

1yd (1m) gold cord with tasselled end

20 x 3in (50 x 7.5cm) woven braid

1 *Cut a strip of mounting (matting) board measuring 20 x 3in (50 x 7.5cm). Join into a ring with staples, overlapping the ends by ¹⁄₂in (12mm). Cover the inside with the printed lining fabric, gluing it in place with PVA (white) glue.*

2 *Sew the pink silk along the short edge with a narrow seam. Press flat, then fold the fabric in half lengthways and press. Slip the circle of fabric over the board, pin the lower edge in place and even out the fullness. Overstitch to the ring, using small stitches which pass through the top of the lining, without sewing through the board.*

3 *Sew the brass rings 2in (5cm) from the top, spacing them evenly, and thread through the fine cord. Sew the gold silk dupion together along the short sides. Run a gathering thread along one edge and pull up to fit around the ring. Distribute the gathers evenly and with the join on the inside, sew to the lower edge of the board.*

4 *Draw up the bottom of the bag tightly, push the raw edges to the inside and firmly sew on the tassel.* ◀

5 *Cut the tasselled cord in half, and sew one piece to either side of the board ring to form a handle. Unravel the last 1in (2.5cm) of cord so that it will lie flat. Cover the ring by coating the braid with a thin layer of PVA glue. Turn under ½in (12mm) at one end, then pin in place, pulling the lower edge tightly over the gathers. When the glue is dry, stitch the braid at the top and bottom.* ▶

Sweet Hearts

The heart is the ultimate symbol of devotion, so heart-shaped gifts have a special significance, whether they are given to friends and family, or exchanged by lovers. These padded hearts are made from leftovers of old lace fabric, embellished with tiny beads and gauzy ribbons. The golden versions are filled with pot-pourri and edged with metallic lace, giving an antique richness.

Materials:

silk backing fabric

small pieces of lace fabric

matching sewing thread

polyester stuffing

rocaille embroidery beads

20 x 1in (50 x 2.5cm) lace

1yd x 1½in (1m x 4cm) gauze ribbon

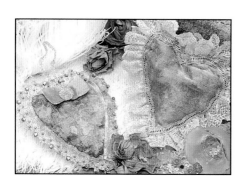

1 Cut out two hearts from backing fabric and one from lace allowing ½in (12mm) all round.

2 Pin the three hearts together, sandwiching the lace heart between the layers of silk. Sew together along one straight side, leaving a 1½in (4cm) gap for turning through.

3 Turn the heart the right way out and stuff firmly, making sure that the stuffing fills out the point of the heart. Slip stitch the sides together, making sure the fabric lies flat with no wrinkles.

4 Sew the beads on to the lace, picking out and highlighting the various designs within the pattern of lace itself.

5 Gather the length of lace to fit around the outside edge of the heart and stitch in place.

6 Cut a 12in (30cm) length of gauze ribbon and sew to the top of the heart to form a hanging loop. Make a bow from the rest of the ribbon and sew to the base of the loop.

Double Heart Basket

*T*his romantic flower basket, made from two interlocking hearts, is an intriguing present. The basic shape is moulded from fine wire mesh and covered in moss to give it a fresh and natural appearance. One heart is packed with roses and the other piled high with strawberries for a summertime treat – once the fruit has been eaten the basket could be filled with pot-pourri or small treasures.

Materials:

chicken wire

pliers

dried sphagnum moss

glue gun

florist's foam

large bunch of dried roses

fresh strawberries

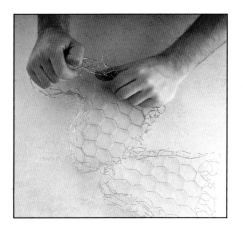

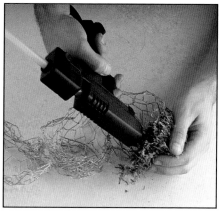

1 *Cut a 12 x 24in (30 x 60cm) piece of chicken wire. Half-way along, cut about 3in (7.5cm) into the wire at both top and bottom. Carefully mould the wire into 2 hearts, bending the mesh over to form a point at the bottom and 2 curves at the top. It may be a good idea to wear gardening gloves while doing this.*

2 *Cover the hearts with moss, a handful at a time, using a glue gun to fix it in place. Press the moss right into the mesh so that all of the wire is covered without losing the outline.*

3 *From the florist's foam, cut a heart shape to fit inside the left-hand heart. Use the glue gun to stick the foam in place. Snip off the dried rose heads and, one at a time, push a line of flowers into the edge of the foam.*

4 *Fill the centre space with more roses, placing them close together to form a padded cushion-like effect. Just before presentation, fill the second heart with fresh strawberries.*

Finishing Touches

First impressions mean a lot, so the way in which a gift is presented is very important. When time and care have gone into making the present itself, equal attention should be given to its wrappings. The examples given here make use of a wide range of materials, from traditional brown parcel paper, corrugated cardboard, string and sealing wax, to delicate silk flowers, dried roses and mulberry papers.

Wrapping and Ribbons

It is always a pleasure to receive a beautifully decorated parcel and the anticipation of unwrapping the package adds much to the excitement of receiving a gift. The thought involved in selecting the perfect paper, ribbons and gift tag to decorate a present is much appreciated, even when the wrappings are all torn off in the haste to find the gift inside.

Until recently, there was only a limited range of commercially printed papers available in the shops. Seasonally patterned Christmas papers appeared at the end of the year, and simple floral and patterned wrapping had to serve for other gifts. Nowadays, however, there are all kinds of attractive papers to choose from; including specific designs for occasions such as christenings, anniversaries and Mother's Day. These are frequently available with co-ordinating ribbons and gift tags.

CREATIVE WRAPPING

For a really personal touch, it is not difficult to come up with some new ideas. Ordinary brown parcel paper and white cartridge (drawing) paper can be decorated to make them into something very original. Gingham checks can be painted in ink or watercolour, and specially bought rubber stamps, old printing type or Indian textile blocks can be used to print a repeated design. Paper doilies or stencils cut from folded paper make Christmas snowflake designs when used with a stencil brush.

Above: Sealing wax was once used as a security device to ensure that letters were not read before they reached their destination. The melted wax was stamped with the sender's personal seal, which cracked when the envelope was opened.

Individually handmade papers can be bought for a luxurious present. Florentine printed papers from Italy are famous for their designs, and a range of delicate tissue-like mulberry papers from the Far East has recently become available. Some of these have tiny flecks of gold and silver leaf.

Some papers are ideally suited to a special kind of gift – a sheet of marbled paper would be a good choice to wrap a book – however, such wrappings do not have to be expensive: left-over fabric from a project could be used to make a matching bow to decorate the parcel or box that contains it. If a gift is an awkward shape, it can be disguised by wrapping it in layers of coloured tissue paper and placing it inside a box, which is then covered in wrapping paper. This can either be a box recycled from a previous occasion or a special presentation box which can be kept afterwards and used for another purpose.

A wide range of paper-based gift ribbons is available and there are colours to match every paper imaginable. These can be formed into curls to make attractive streamers to festoon a package. Satin ribbons look luxurious and paper ribbon, which comes in string-like form, can be unravelled and tied into extravagant bows. Wire-edged ribbon is ideal for making stylish bows, as it can be gently twisted into different effects and will keep its shape.

Below: These découpage boxes have been covered with reproduction scraps, stuck down with wallpaper paste and finished with a craquelure-effect varnish to give them a period feel. They would make perfect containers for tiny presents.

Above: There are now specialist dealers in ephemera; old greetings cards, postcards, scraps, tickets, labels and other paper items, all of which can be used as decoration.

Above: These small, elaborate envelopes with cord and tassel fastenings are made in India. Larger versions are also made, often in brown paper and lined with sari fabric.

Above: A home-made parcel label.

Above: Bows, ribbons, cords, scraps and tissue papers, grouped together, can provide inspiration for many different ways to wrap up a gift.

Parcels

*T*hese four ways of wrapping up a parcel are inspiring and different. Choose a theme to suit the person who will be receiving the present – a gift for a gardener could be bound with green twine, or the large shell parcel could contain a souvenir of a seaside holiday. Several small boxes, covered in different papers, then bundled together with ribbon, make a package that is almost too good to unwrap.

HEART PARCEL

Materials:

handmade writing paper

double-sided sticky tape

scraps of gold card (cardboard)

PVA (white) glue

narrow white parcel ribbon

1 Cover the boxes with writing paper in toning colours, carefully mitring the corners and sticking ends down with double-sided sticky tape.

2 Decorate the corner of each box with a decorative scrap, or cut hearts from gold card (cardboard), gluing them down with PVA (white) glue. Stack the packages together and tie up with ribbon.

GOLDEN SUN PARCEL

Materials:

gold tissue paper

gold- and silver-flecked mulberry paper

card (cardboard) with sun motif

narrow gold parcel ribbon

1 Wrap the box up with several layers of gold tissue paper, ensuring any writing on the box does not show through. Cover the parcel with mulberry paper, trimming the overlapping edges to make a neat mitre.

2 Place the sun motif card on top of the parcel, and tie around with gold parcel ribbon.

Rose Parcel

Materials:

tissue paper

pressed flowers

handmade paper with petals

garden twine

sealing wax

dried roses

gift tag

1 *Cover the box with several layers of tissue paper. Scatter pressed flowers on the top before wrapping around the handmade paper.*

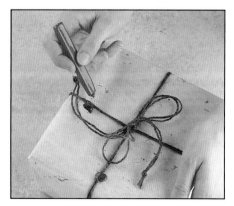

2 *Tie a double length of garden twine around the parcel, finishing off with a bow. Drip sealing wax on to the string to hold it in place.*

3 *Tuck three dried roses under the string and tie a gift tag on to the bow.*

Shell Parcel

Materials:

tissue paper

PVA (white) glue

shell-printed scraps

shell-printed wrapping paper

thick natural twine

abalone shell

1 Cover the box with several sheets of tissue paper and stick shell-printed scraps on to the top layer, before covering with wrapping paper.

2 Tie a length of twine around the parcel, finishing with a bow.

3 Cut a piece of twine and thread it through the shell. Tie the shell on to the parcel.

Gift Tags

These labels combine the natural textures of handmade paper, raffia and twine with familiar office stationery – paper fasteners and reinforcement rings. They are easily assembled from offcuts of paper and card, decorated with printed scraps and pressed flowers. With the recipient's name written in gold ink, a special gift tag is the perfect way to personalize an elegantly wrapped parcel.

Materials:

2 sheets of handmade papers in different colours

ruler

craft knife

brass paper fasteners

printed scraps

hole punch

reinforcement rings

raffia

1 Tear a rectangle measuring about 3 x 3½in (7.5 x 9cm) from the darker paper. To do this, hold a ruler down on the paper and pull the paper against the ruler. This will give a soft deckle edge to the tag but will ensure a reasonably square shape.

2 With a craft knife, cut a second rectangle, ½in (12mm) smaller all round than the first.

3 Fix the two pieces of paper together with brass paper fasteners in three of the corners, as shown. Stick a small printed scrap, or cut-out picture, in the fourth corner. ◀

4 Make a hole in one corner with a hole punch and stick a reinforcement ring on the back. Make a tie from a short length of raffia and loop it through the hole. ▶

Presentation Boxes

A beautifully decorated box is a stylish way to conceal a surprise present. Awkwardly shaped gifts, or a selection of small parcels will all fit into a lidded box, which can then be used afterwards. Natural materials work well with fabric flowers; the oval box is tied up with paper ribbon, and the round box is covered with brown paper, surrounded with flowers and encircled with raffia.

Materials:

paper ribbon

oval cardboard box

PVA (white) glue

corrugated cardboard

selection of fabric flowers

1 Cut a length of paper ribbon, long enough to fit around the rim of the box lid with a small overlap. Unfurl the ribbon and fix in place with PVA (white) glue, folding and gluing down the surplus ribbon under and above the rim. The top of the lid will be covered.

2 Draw around the lid on to corrugated cardboard and cut out the oval. Glue on to the lid to cover the surplus ribbon.

3 Cut and unfurl two lengths of ribbon, 3 times the width of the lid. Glue to each side, tucking the end under the rim.

4 Tie the ribbon in a large bow and arrange the loops neatly. Cut the ends into a "V" shape or at an angle.

5 Put the lid on the box. Measure the distance from the bottom edge to the bottom of the rim of the lid. Cut a strip of corrugated cardboard this width, and long enough to wrap around the box. Glue in place.

6 Cut the fabric flowers and leaves from their wire stalks and glue on to the box, to give the effect of a sheaf of flowers under the bow.

CHRISTENING
GOWN

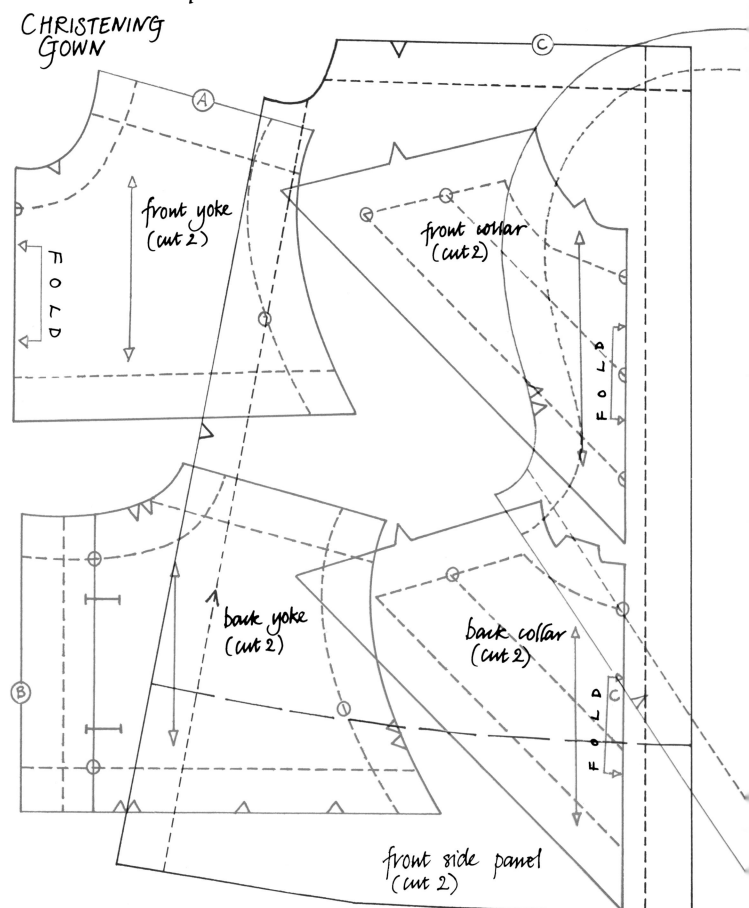

Ⓐ

front yoke
(cut 2)

F O L D

Ⓒ

front collar
(cut 2)

F O L D

back yoke
(cut 2)

Ⓑ

back collar
(cut 2)

F O L D

C

F O L D

front side panel
(cut 2)

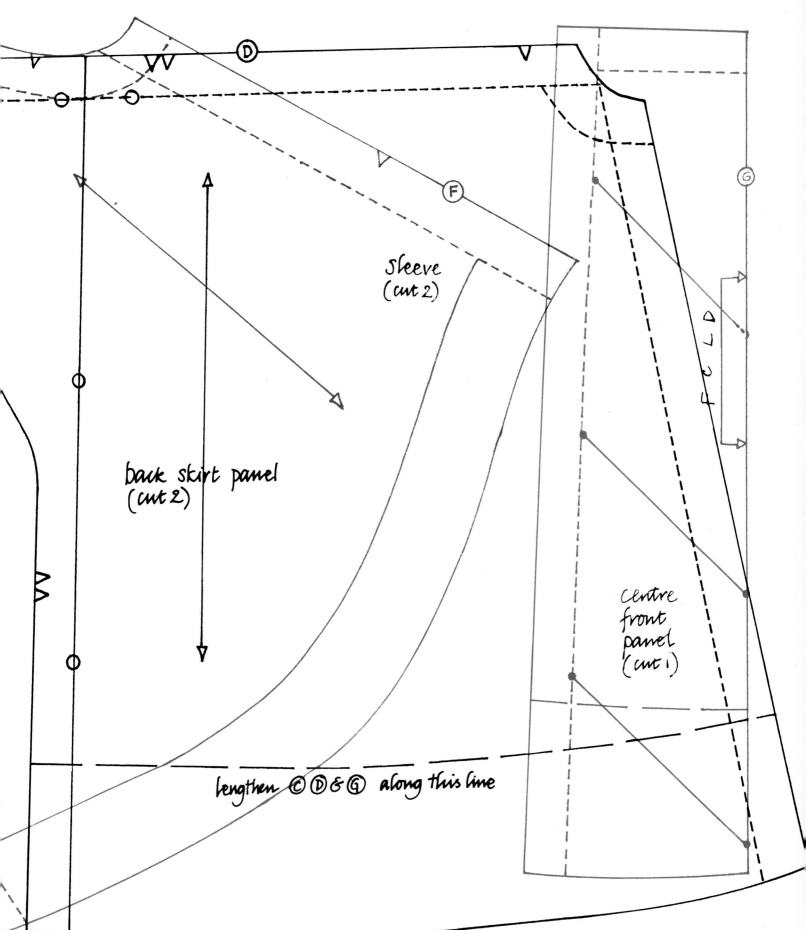

Ⓓ

Ⓕ

Ⓖ

F
O
L
D

Sleeve
(cut 2)

back skirt panel
(cut 2)

centre
front
panel
(cut 1)

lengthen Ⓒ Ⓓ & Ⓖ along this line

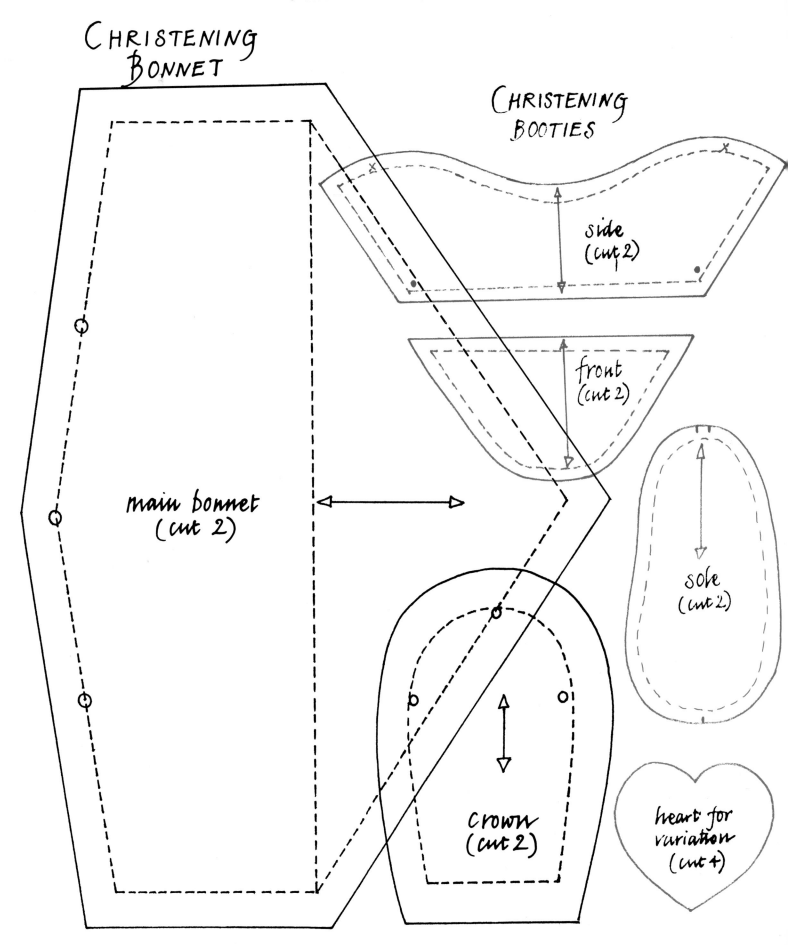

CHRISTENING BONNET

CHRISTENING BOOTIES

side (cut 2)

front (cut 2)

sole (cut 2)

main bonnet (cut 2)

crown (cut 2)

heart for variation (cut 4)

Calico Doll

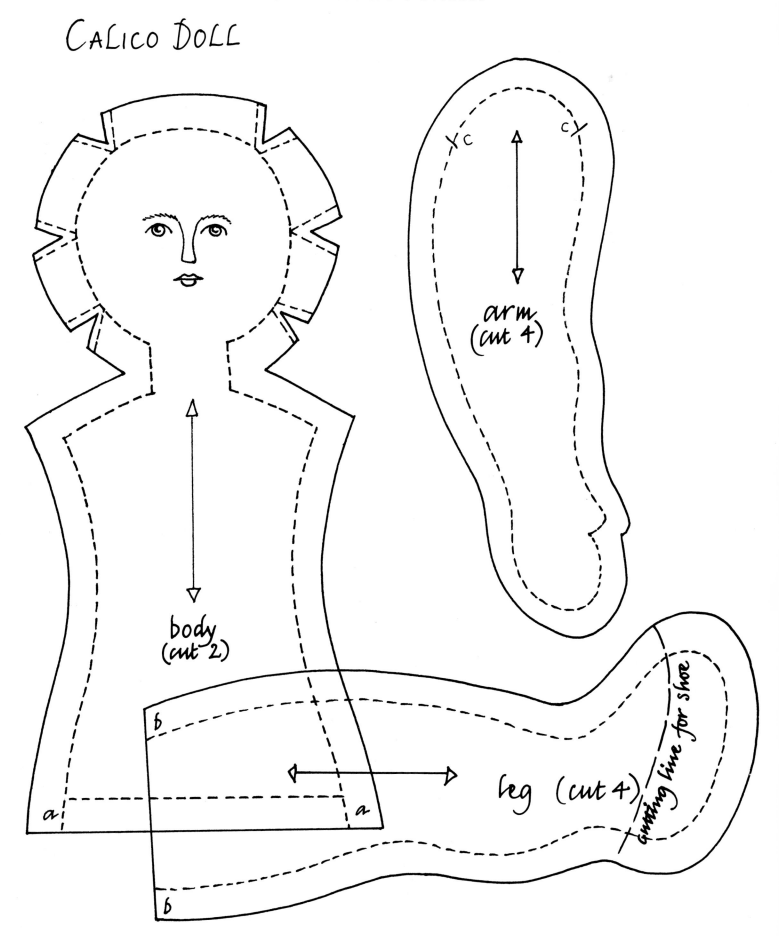

arm
(cut 4)

body
(cut 2)

leg (cut 4)

cutting line for shoe

CALICO DOLL

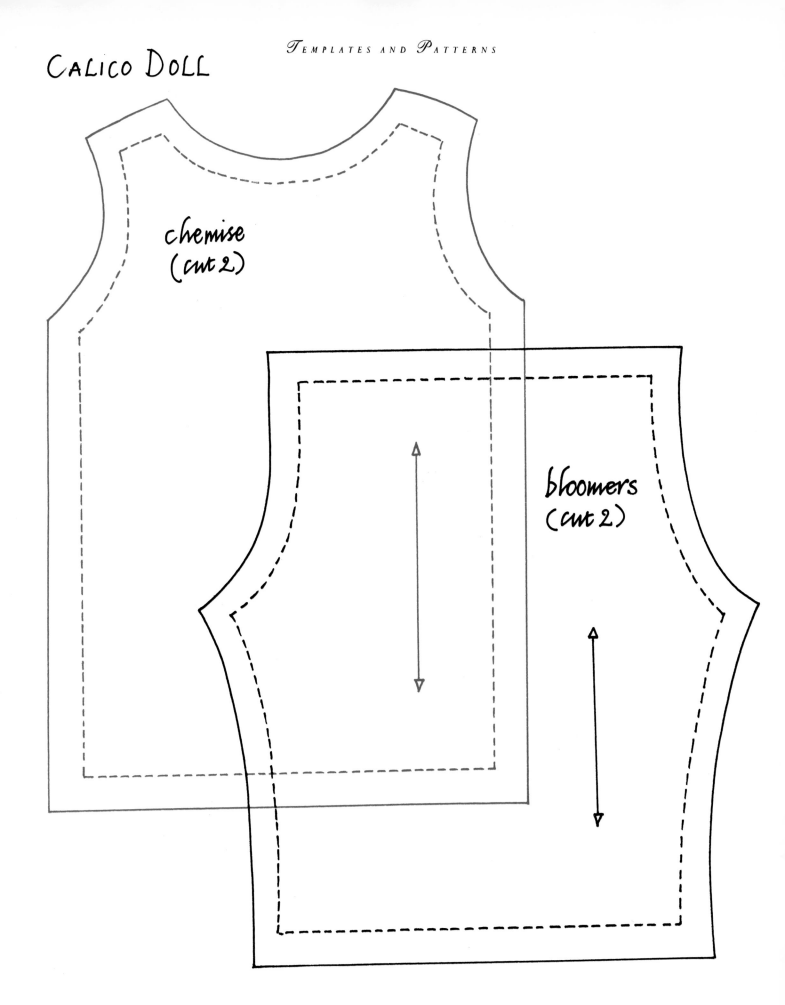

chemise
(cut 2)

bloomers
(cut 2)

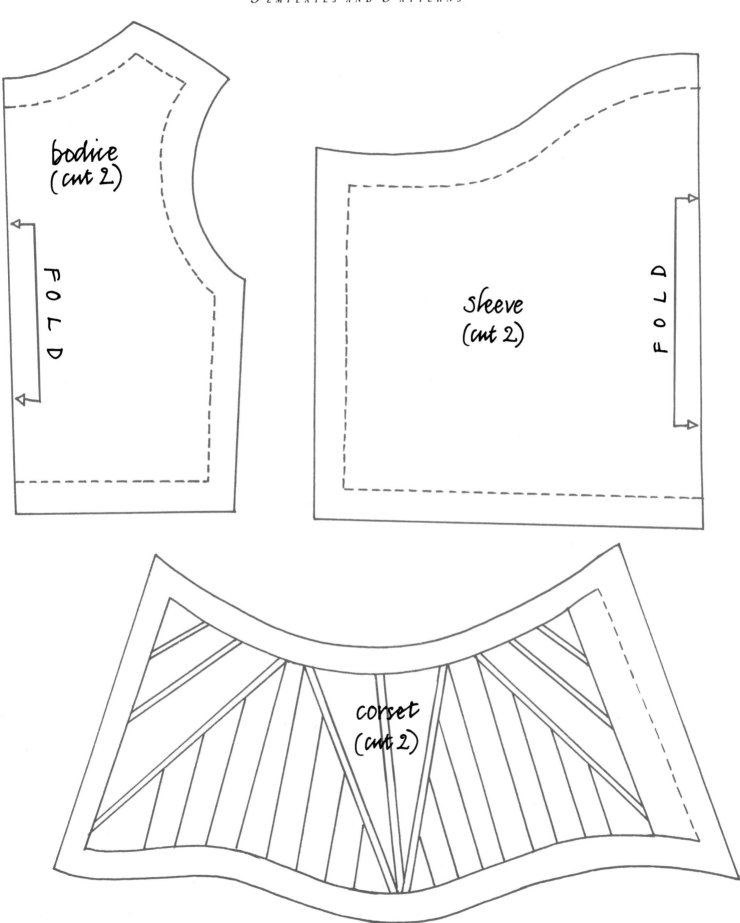

bodice
(cut 2)

F O L D

sleeve
(cut 2)

F O L D

corset
(cut 2)

WEDDING QUILT

quilt border

pansy template

Hand Towel & Washcloth

Techniques

$\mathcal{T}$he basic skills of traditional sewing rely on a methodical approach. They are easy to learn and, with practice, will give a professional look to any piece of needlework. Careful pressing of the piece at each stage will also help to ensure a good appearance.

CLIPPING AND TURNING CURVES

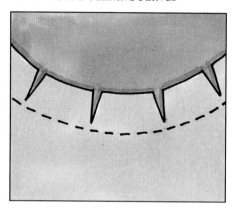

When joining curved edges, a neat finish is achieved by clipping the excess fabric so that the seam can lie flat. If the seam allowance lies on the inside (above) it should be clipped at regular intervals almost to the stitch line.

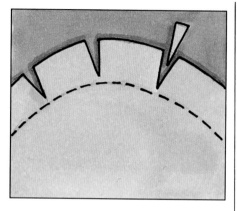

For an outside curve (above) small "V" shaped notches are snipped out. On a sharp curve the outside edge of the surplus fabric may be trimmed back slightly. Press the seam over to one side with a cool iron, then press it open.

MITRING CORNERS

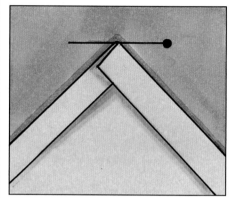

The hems on right-angled corners are finished off by mitring. Turn under the edges of the fabric along both edges and press, then turn under the seam allowance and press. Mark the corner with a pin.

TACKING (BASTING)

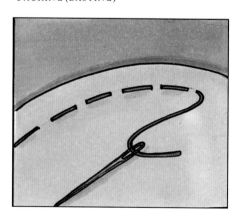

This is a temporary stitch, used to hold seams together before sewing by machine. The stitches should be between ¼in (5mm) and ⅜in (1cm) long and evenly spaced. Use a contrasting thread to make the stitching easy to unpick.

MACHINE APPLIQUÉ

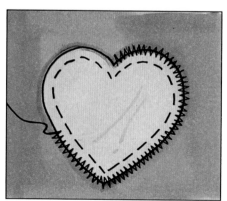

Machine appliqué is quick and hardwearing. Cut out the motif, then pin and tack (baste) in position on the main fabric. Set the sewing machine to a close zig zag or satin stitch and sew around the edges of the shape so that the raw edges are covered completely and will not fray.

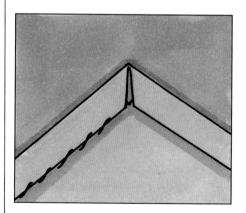

Unfold the sides, leaving the raw edges turned under. Fold the corner inwards so that the pin lies on the outside edge. Refold the side, turnings over the corner, and slip stitch in place.

Transferring markings with tailor's tacks

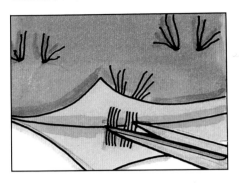

This is the most accurate way to transfer markings from a paper pattern onto double fabric. With the pattern still pinned in place, make a tiny slit across the symbol to be marked. Using a double thread, tack several loops through both layers. Remove the pattern, gently ease the fabric apart, and cut the loops. The tufts of thread mark the joining points.

Transferring markings with dressmaker's carbon

Dressmaker's carbon is used to transfer an embroidery design from paper onto smooth fabric. Use light paper for dark-coloured fabrics and dark for light fabrics. Place the carbon-side down between the drawing and fabric, secure in place and draw over the outline with a pencil, pressing firmly to mark through on to the fabric.

Transferring markings with a dressmaker's pen

Special felt-tip pens with either a water soluble ink or one which fades with time are ideal for transferring embroidery or quilting designs, as they leave no trace. They can be used to draw freehand onto the main fabric or to draw round a cut-out template.

Stitches

There are many different embroidery stitches, some elaborate and intricate, others straightforward to work. The following stitches are used throughout this book, and each have a special purpose and provide the basic vocabulary of decorative stitching.

Back stitch

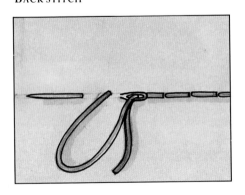

Back stitch produces a strong seam which is an alternative to machine stitching. It produces an unbroken line, suitable for outlining designs, and is worked in small regular stitches.

Blanket stitch

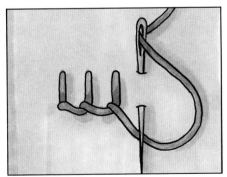

Blanket stitch may be used for finishing hems and, when the stitches are worked close together, for buttonholes. It is used decoratively for scalloped edging. Work from left to right, bringing the needle down vertically and looping the thread under its tip before pulling through.

Chain stitch

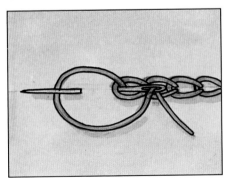

Chain stitch is used for outlining and for filling in spaces when worked in close rows or a spiral. The thread is looped under the needle's tip and held down as the needle is drawn through the ground fabric. The needle is then pushed back through the hole it left to form the next stitch.

CROSS STITCH

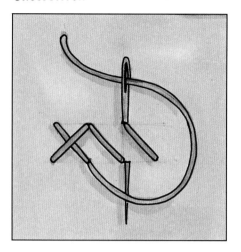

Cross stitch is the best known of all embroidery stitches; it was used by the ancient Egyptians and more recently for the samplers made by nineteenth-century schoolchildren. It is worked in two parts, and the top stitches should always lie in the same direction. The stitches can be worked singly, or built up in rows, as shown.

FEATHER STITCH

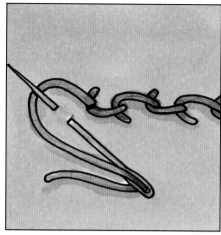

Feather stitch is a looped stitch, traditionally used for smocking and decorating crazy patchwork. It can be worked in straight or curved lines. Bring the thread through the fabric and make slanting stitches, working alternately to the right and left of the line to be covered.

FRENCH KNOT

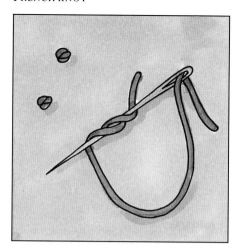

French knots are used sparingly as accents, or worked more closely together to produce a texture. The stitch should be worked with the fabric in a frame, leaving both hands free. Bring the thread through and hold down. Twist the thread around the needle a few times and tighten. Holding the thread taught, insert the needle back into the fabric with the other hand, at the point from which it emerged. Pull the needle through the thread twists to form the knot.

SATIN STITCH

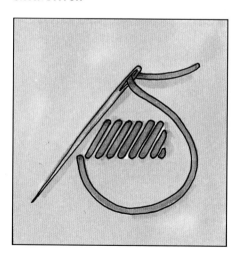

Satin stitch is used for filling in and outlining. Ensure the fabric is always held tautly in a frame to prevent puckering. Carry the thread across the area to be filled, then return it back underneath the fabric as near as possible to the point from which the needle emerged.

SLIP STITCH

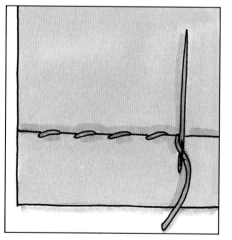

Slip stitch is used to join together two folded edges, and for flat-hemming a turned-in edge. It should be nearly invisible. Pick up two threads of the single fabric and slip the needle through the fold for about ¼in (5mm). Draw the thread through to make a tiny stitch.

STEM STITCH

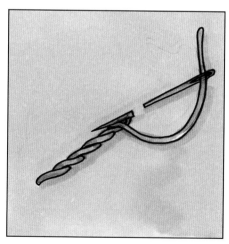

Stem stitch is also known as crewel stitch and is widely used for filling, outlining and shading. The stitches should be kept even, working upwards with the thread to the right side of the needle.

CROSS STITCH ALPHABET

Contributors

$\mathcal{T}$he author and publishers would like to thank the following for creating items for photography. Many of these designers are happy to accept commissions. All other projects were designed and made by Lucinda Ganderton.

Deirdre Hawken and **Gudrun Luckett**
35 Glenluce Road
London SE3 7SD

Drawstring bag pp 32–5. Scarves designed by Deirdre Hawken, courtesy of Adel Roostein Ltd.

McQueens Flowers
11–15 Great Eastern Street
London EC2A 3ET
071 247 4792

Lavender wreath pp 66–7; rose and lavender posy pp 122–3; double heart basket pp 130–1; pp 110 and 111 bottom

Abigail Mill
Studio 10
Muspole Workshops
25–27 Muspole Street
Norwich
Norfolk NR3 1DG

Valentine pp 124–5

Cheryl Owen
Studio 117
31 Clerkenwell Close
London EC1R 0AT

Christening booties pp 104–5

Isabel Stanley
5 Herne Hill Mansions
Herne Hill
SE24 9QN

Jewellery roll pp 62–5; wedding quilt pp 82–3; scented cushions pp 118–121

Isabella Whitworth
4 Kingfisher Close
Abingdon, Oxon
OX14 5NP

Jewellery box pp 54–7; lace handkerchief pp 58–9; hand towel and washcloth pp 72–3

Dorothy Wood
8 Orchard Close
Osgathorpe
Loughborough
Leicester LE12 9UF

Pouch bag pp 36–7; christening gown pp 98–101; christening bonnet pp 102–3

Index

ACKNOWLEDGEMENTS

The author and publishers would like to thank
the following for lending materials for
photography.

Helen Banzhaff
31 Lampmead Road
London SE12 8QJ

Embroidered cushion p 50

Cold Christmas Designs
94 The Maltings
Stanstead Abbotts
Herts. SG12 8HG
tel: 0920 871876

pp 6, 7, 96 and 128 bottom left

Rosemary L. Dunley
Christening Heritage
The Dove Cote
5 Wilmcote Grove
Ainsdale
Southport PR8 2SP
tel: 01704 574 511
(Please send £1.00 for brochure)

pp 94, 95 bottom right

Trousseau of Nottingham Lace
Unit J
14–18 St Mary's Gate
The Lace Market
Nottingham NG1 1PF
tel: 0602 483980

pp 6, 7, 48, 77 right and 96

Claire Norwood who made the wedding
shoes on p 77 for Claire Thorogood.

Georgia Vienna Ltd
18–20 Greatness Road
Sevenoaks
Kent TN14 5BY
tel: 0732 740194

p 22 bottom left

A special thanks to **Emma Ganderton** for
lending numerous props for styling, and for
her continual support throughout the project.